Archie Jackson

CRICKET'S TRAGIC GENIUS

The Slattery Media Group Pty Ltd

902/31 Spring Street, Melbourne

Victoria, Australia, 3000

Visit: *slatterymedia.com*

Published by The Slattery Media Group, 2020

COVER: **Archie Jackson in full flight:** "He steps forward to cover-drive...the stroke is perfectly balanced and true...the bat seems to be a whip in his hands."—A.R.B. Palmer, Daily Guardian. Image ©Getty Images.

 A catalogue record for this book is available from the National Library of Australia

Group Publisher: Geoff Slattery

Editors: Russell Jackson, Geoff Slattery

General and project manager: Jeffrey Sickert

Art Direction, Cover Design and Typeset: Kate Slattery

Printed in Australia by McPherson's Printing Group

Archie Jackson

CRICKET'S TRAGIC GENIUS

DAVID FRITH

The Classic Biography, Revised & Updated

www.slatterymedia.com

Archie Jackson: Balmain historian Cliff Winning wrote of Jackson: "He was one of the most lovable characters to ever don cricketing attire..."

For my beloved Debbie (1940–2019)
for the last time.

In that short life
there was abundant action
and a full measure of joy.

A.G. (JOHNNIE) MOYES, (1893-1963)

Archie Jackson

Contents

Jackson in the nets: "...artistry, enhanced by a beguiling touch of self-consciousness..."

EDITOR'S NOTE

In *Frith's Encounters* (Von Krumm Publishing, 2014), one of the dozens of David Frith books that grace the shelves of true cricket lovers around the world, often there is a scene familiar to ardent fans of this revered historian and author. Scaling the steps outside the home of some ancient hero of the game, Frith enters an Aladdin's cave of team photographs and dusty trophies, and soon the precious memories from faraway fields start spilling across the page. Off the reader drifts, eased into a lost world.

With a similar mixture of anticipation and boyish enthusiasm as Frith, in March of 2019, I paced through London's Waterloo station and jumped aboard a train bound for Guildford, in deepest Surrey, armed with a few cricket magazines and instructions to keep my eyes peeled for a waiting Ford Escort (complete with Ken Barrington's initials on the numberplate). Sure enough, up pulled the car, driven by the man whose cricket publications have inspired a greater love and deeper understanding of the game for so many of us.

Frith, now three lofted drives from a century himself, might not enjoy the comparison to such antique figures, but like Australia's 1920s idol Jack Gregory as the author found him in 1970s Narooma, and countless other heroes profiled in Frith's lengthy career, he presented much older and greyer that day in Guildford than the man whose face, words and force of nature led *Wisden Cricket Monthly*—under his editorship, the game's most engaging and re-readable magazine. But it was, and is, time to take stock of his life in the game, and such appraisals are better done during life's evening session. In person, Frith was no less chatty, charming and warm than his written self, his enthusiasm to talk cricket and cricketers undiminished, his assessments as peppery and shrewd as ever.

At Frith's home, one feels like a pilgrim. No sooner are guests through the door then they're escorted into his library—more accurately a shrine to cricket—an idiosyncratic and overwhelming labyrinth of books and objects. Leant against one bookcase, unmistakable to the eye and seeming to harbour mystical qualities once it's placed in the visitor's hands, is a bat used by Archie Jackson, the alluring subject of this book.

Forty-five years on from the acclaimed first arrival of Archie Jackson's story, David Frith's ongoing devotion to the man is reflective of a lifetime in thrall of cricket and those players who made it that little bit more romantic and special. The stylists and poets. The gentlemen. But you will read enough about the dreamy and doomed Archie in the pages that follow. First it pays to consider the service to the game of Frith, the self-described "cricket slave", the indefatigable historian, prolific storyteller and keeper of flames.

Picking a favourite among his books is impossible in view of their breadth and variety. Contenders to join *Archie* on the podium are *Pageant of Cricket* (Macmillan, 1987), Frith's monumental survey of cricket pictures, and *By His Own Hand—a study of cricket's suicides,* (Stanley Paul, 1991), the sort of spooky, dark and engrossing volume only a game as emotionally testing as cricket could prompt, and which only a researcher as committed as Frith could have wrangled. Frith's editorships of *The Cricketer* (1972-78) and *Wisden Cricket Monthly* (1979-96) set a bar nobody else has reached or could hope to reach, the latter the perfect blend of the present and past, shrewdly observed, deftly illustrated, voluble and welcoming, its reportage and opinions delivered with unchallengeable expertise and style.

Of Frith's 1974 study of Archie Jackson, the influential Australian journalist and newspaper editor Rohan Rivett wrote: "Frith has negotiated the fine, dangerous line that separates pathos from bathos. All cricket lovers are in his debt for pinpointing facts unknown or forgotten." That stands as a decent appraisal of Frith's entire body of work: editorial discernment, meticulous research and, at regular intervals, the Eureka moments too often lacking in cricket publishing. We remain in his debt.

As Frith notes, it was with succinct finality that Archie Jackson's headstone pronounced: "He played the game," and although Frith played it too—for Don Bradman's St George and Victor Trumper's Paddington, in Sydney, and enthusiastically in all corners of the world—above all else he has *served* it. Bradman himself put it well: "Thank goodness the cricket world has always thrown up men like David Frith, who seems to regard a contribution to cricket history as a duty to mankind." To encounter Frith's remarkable body of work is to know the man. As this is a bittersweet book, perhaps it is appropriate to conclude on a bittersweet note: cricket will never have a friend as committed, generous and protective as David Frith.

RUSSELL JACKSON
January 2020

FOREWORD

By Harold Larwood
(1904-1995)
Nottinghamshire and England fast bowler

When first approached to write a foreword, I politely refused. However, it was explained by this persistent fellow that he had spent considerable time researching on a cricketer he believed I must have admired. I asked who this could be? His reply left me humbled, for it was none other than Archie Jackson.

It hit me just about as hard as Archie did that day at Adelaide in 1929 when, in his first Test innings for Australia, with 97 runs against his name and having had his back to the wall, he cover-drove me to bring up his hundred. That ball was delivered as fast as any I had ever bowled previously.

That glorious stroke has lived in my memory to this day for its ease and perfect timing. I am sure that few among the many thousands present sighted the ball as it raced to the boundary. I personally had a very great admiration for Archie, and I am sure we "Poms" counted him as one of us. He never failed to congratulate the bowler or fieldsman whenever he was dismissed by a good ball, and at the same time he would be the first to let you know when he thought you were not bowling so well. He would say: "You must have had a late one last night, Harold!"

He was always friendly, no matter the tenseness of the situation—you just had to find a place in your heart for a fellow like him. The respect he showed for others grew on you.

I remember once, in England during the 1930 series, in scoring 73 at The Oval in the fifth Test, he was taking quite a physical beating. As he came down the wicket to level a high spot or two he said: "Well, Harold, it's only a game, but what a grand one we're having today! I hope you're enjoying our battle as much as those spectators seem to be. You know, you've hit me almost as many times as I've hit you! I wish you'd drop one a little off line occasionally!"

I never knew him to flinch or complain at any time. No, Archie Jackson, like his hero Victor Trumper, was born to be great, and great he was, for he received the same respect from us "Poms" as from his own team.

But we had a feeling that something was amiss with this

young fellow in 1930. Those of us who were closely associated with him knew that the English climate did not suit him; he was not himself. He still batted with the same charm that only he was capable of, but it was apparent that he was not the same Archie as that of 1928-29.

One of my most cherished possessions to this day is a personal telegram sent to me by Archie while undoubtedly a very sick boy in Brisbane; it congratulated me on my bowling in that controversial Test of 1933. At the time he must have been very close to meeting his Maker, but he was still conscious enough to remember an old friend.

I remember also a number of us Englishmen visiting Archie in the private hospital in Brisbane one afternoon after practice before the fourth Test. It was the last time we were to see him, for during the final stages of that Test match he passed away. We felt the depression that was cast over the ground when early that morning the news came through that Archie was no more.

It was hard to believe. We knew that our loss was Australia's too. Privileged were those who had known him. I for one could never forget Archie Jackson.

HAROLD LARWOOD

(Foreword written by Harold Larwood for the 1974 edition)

*'Tis certain I shall never
recover if I am to be long
separate from you.
Illness is a long lane,
but I see you at
the end of it.*

JOHN KEATS (1795-1821)

CHAPTER ONE

In the Line
of Trumper

There is love—and often sadness—at the heart of a cult. Victor Trumper was the first tragic hero of Australian cricket. His failing health robbed him of untold hours in the sun, and although his death in 1915 did not shorten his international career, the loss of his maturity, the years of fullness when a veteran spreads himself in relaxation and reminiscence, were denied him. He was humble and kind. He deserved a long life. All who knew him believed this.

The dreamy Alan Kippax, whose beautiful strokeplay often mirrored Trumper's, had a broad and loyal following during the 1920s and 1930s, but in an era when his finesse was mistrusted by Test selectors he left his lyrical style in the collective memory as his stature was undeservedly eroded. His figures, impressive though they remain, tell but one side of his story.

At his zenith Kippax welcomed into the ranks of the New South Wales team a slender, athletic lad who, although he'd never seen Trumper, possessed all the comely movement and keenness of eye of Sydney's God of Cricket. His exceptional talent had revealed itself at a precocious age, and cricketers all around him watched expectantly as Archie Jackson's promised gift emerged.

This was the beginning of a cult. Men of all ages who saw him never forgot him, and a generation later they still held his banner. All those who had made his acquaintance shared the desire to be regarded as his intimate friends.

Jackson was to bear uncomplainingly an insidious sickness that racked him for years. In valiant but misguided optimism he disdained treatment.

The last of the line, he died at 23 (the youngest Test cricketer to die through the first 130 years of Test cricket, until Bangladesh batsman Manjural Islam, 22, was killed in a road accident in Khulna on March 16, 2007). Cricket's transition from an aesthetic exercise to a mere mathematical strategy was under way around that time. Jackson's influence was seriously missed. No spectator could ever have watched him late-cut or advance to the drive without having to stifle the wish to imitate.

In such premature death there is a danger that the legend becomes over-gilded. That is not the case here. A wealth of evidence delineates Archie Jackson's genius and his youthful splendour.

The wider tragedy, apart from the pity that avid England only ever saw a faint shadow of the man, is that during the businesslike 1930s there was no Archie Jackson to provide an on-going model of ease and elegance as an inspiration for youthful cricketers in both countries. Kippax, his own mentor, played halfway through the decade and made many enchanting and sizable hundreds, but his peak had been around 1926, when 21 of his 22 Australian caps were still to come. Two savage blows to the head also affected "Kippy" irretrievably.

The decade—for Australia—was dominated by Bradman, Ponsford, Woodfull, and McCabe, all except the last having a predictable near-infallibility. Archie Jackson would surely have continued to add a touch of delicate artistry.

Alternatively, he might have tightened up as the seasons passed, unable, even by repeating his follies, to recapture his artistic youth. But I doubt it. If he had a spiritual descendant, it may well have been the equally elegant Mark Waugh.

A telephone call got things under way: "Bill Hunt, the cricketer?"

"That is so."

I introduced myself. "I understand from Alan Kippax that you were a close friend of Archie Jackson's?"

"May I say that no-one knew him better!"

So began the reconstruction of a career. I pored over Bill's scrapbooks, and filled my notebooks as reminiscence played itself out. He introduced me to Jackson's two sisters, and they in turn referred me to his former fiancée. I began to see the subject from other angles.

Walking the streets of Balmain, standing outside his childhood home, talking with elder sister Peggie in the house in Drummoyne to which the family later graduated, finding

Archie Jackson's grave at the Field of Mars Cemetery, seeking out old team-mates and adversaries—I found that the young man's spirit lived on quite powerfully.

Unexpectedly, I obtained access to a number of Jackson's letters, most of them full of hope and rationalisation, written with candour to some of his friends during the last five years of his life.

Then, finally, Bill Hunt arranged to show a brief cine-film of Archie Jackson demonstrating his range of strokes on the No.2 Ground at Sydney over forty summers earlier. There he stood, bat held high on the handle, his cap-peak drooping like a guardsman's.

The casual elegance of his leg glances, the whalebone suppleness of his wrists as he steered the ball square and backward, the lightness of footwork, the ballet-like inclination of the body as he cover-drove: all this artistry, enhanced by a beguiling touch of self-consciousness, burned a vivid impression on my mind.

The demonstration had been more than adequate. The only surviving film of Victor Trumper batting is an abrupt misrepresentation of his magical technique, but for five enchanted minutes I had had the great good fortune to see a faithful image of his spiritual young descendant. I found myself aligned with all those thousands who, having seen Archie Jackson batting, sighed for more as he left the field of play.

I pleaded with Bill Hunt to run the film again. He fiddled with the 16mm projector, but in vain. There was a technical problem. It was as if I were being told: you can't see Archie any more, just as his legions of fans were denied him from 1932 onwards.

CHAPTER TWO

Emigrant Boy

Like Adam Lindsay Gordon, "Little Digger" Billy Hughes, Russell Drysdale, Frank Ifield, Patrick White, Charlie Bannerman and quite a few other famous Australians, Archie Jackson was born on the opposite side of the world. The Jackson family lived at 1 Anderson Place, Rutherglen, south of Glasgow, when Archibald arrived on September 5, 1909. Margaret and Alexander already had two daughters: Lil, aged five, and Peggie, three.

"Sandy" (father Alex) was manager of a brickworks at Belvedere. He had been taken to Australia in a sailing ship with his parents when he was twelve, but returned to Scotland five or six years later. Now, as a 41-year-old working man with responsibilities, he eyed New South Wales thoughtfully. Times were tough in Glasgow.

Thus Sandy struck out again for Australia and paved the way

for Mrs Jackson and the children to follow eighteen months later. *Themistocles*, soon to be sunk in the First World War, landed them safely in Sydney on August 1, 1913.

The family set up house in the tilting, rambling old harbourside suburb of Balmain: at 14 Ferdinand Street, a small, cosy, iron-roofed, terraced house, built in two storeys of brick, with a laced-iron balcony. It still stands.

After the War the family was completed by the birth of Jeanie, a precious sister for the other girls, and for Archie, whose early disapproval at not getting a baby brother soon evaporated. "Don't leave her outside in the pram!" he often pleaded. "Someone'll take her away!" He spoilt Jeanie more with each passing year.

There was never much money about, and Archie had to make do with one pair of pants for the greater part of his boyhood, the sole advantage being that his mother could withhold them whenever he was forbidden to go out.

But the home felt secure and was happy. Sandy worked at Cockatoo Dockyard and gave the rest of his time to his family. He put rubber bars on Archie's worn shoes to serve as soccer boots. He made a bat for him to use in the street games, both by day and under the illumination of the gas lamps: not merely a carved plank, but a realistically-shaped implement with a *cane handle*. He earned a tender adulation in return.

"Isn't that your boy, Sandy?" said a workmate one afternoon as a rowing boat floated past the Dock with a small figure lying face-down to avoid recognition. The lad explained that evening that he had only wanted to see his Dad at work. The punishment for truancy was not severe.

The parents usually remained good-humoured even when he returned with a sackful of apples filched from the orchard up at Mars Field. Other times he amused himself by hitching a ride on the laundry cart through the narrow Balmain streets.

A well-remembered crisis was when he fought with schoolmate Tommy Thompson through four consecutive afternoons before sister Lil felt bound to tell Mum, who went straight down to Birchgrove Park to break it up. Even though he grew into a gentleman, he was never anybody's pushover.

He was no angel, but he was loving, and he was greatly loved. When Archie's school, Birchgrove, played cricket against Smith Street, he met Bill Hunt and began a lifelong friendship. They became pals during the 1920-21 season, when J.W.H.T. Douglas's MCC team was moving round Australia from one defeat to the next at the mighty hands of Warwick Armstrong, Jack Gregory, Ted McDonald, Charlie Macartney, Herby Collins, Charlie Kelleway, "Nip" Pellew, and Arthur Mailey—a formidable collection of skills.

Archie idolised certain cricketers from each side, and he and Bill—when they were not playing "numbers cricket" out of a hymn-book in Bible class—had a resourceful manoeuvre for getting to the Sydney Cricket Ground. They "wagged" school at lunchtime, hopped on to a Wood Coffill hearse on its way back to the city, and used their threepence lunch money to get into the ground, where they quenched their thirsts at the bubbler at the base of the Hill, watched the international stars at play—dreaming of playing out there too—and went hungry.

After play they usually hitched a ride on the meat wagon back to Balmain, where the mothers strove to fill their bellies.

"They talk about pollution in the 1970s!" growled Bill Hunt fifty years later. "In those days the people of Balmain used to spread coal dust on their bread!"

Archie's special capabilities in the field of sport soon became obvious. He was selected for New South Wales Schoolboys at both soccer and cricket, travelling to Melbourne under Wendell Bill's captaincy for the summer game and impressing the cricket fraternity there, and distinguishing himself in the inter-state soccer carnival as a slight but highly-skilled centre-forward adept at flicking the ball over the head of a charging opponent and running round him. He played against South Australia twice, Victoria, and Queensland, scoring thirteen goals.

The Jackson home was hardly a hundred yards from Birchgrove Park, where Balmain District Cricket Club played each Saturday (and where Rugby League had been launched in April 1906). Balmain's captain was whimsical Arthur Mailey, plumber, cartoonist, writer, indefatigable and extravagant spinner of the ball for New South Wales and Australia.

Soon after little Archie entered the lower grades, playing in short trousers and appearing too fragile for exposure to adult fast bowling, Mailey wrote prophetically of him in the local paper:

> Balmain has developed a young batsman who may take a big part in Australian cricket. The club officials must be congratulated upon their success. May other clubs have the same good fortune. It is not often that we see a fifteen-year-old batsman—for he was fifteen two weeks ago—with such a splendid variety of strokes as A. Jackson, the boy cricketer, who scored 71 for Balmain against the juniors last Saturday.

As a rule, in a boy so young, there is that apparent anxiety that affects his cricket, and periods of cramped play occasionally are seen. But Jackson just moves along, flicking this ball past point or through the covers and turning the next sweetly to leg with the grace of a master. As a second line of defence, his legs are always in a handy position, but it is refreshing to know that he intends to use his bat whenever possible.

I am not going to compare him with the glorious Victor Trumper at this stage, but if a wealth of common sense and ability is an asset, then this boy's future is assured. He played with the Balmain 2nds last season, and should find a place in the first team this year.

As a second string in his bow he has the moral support of twelve juvenile barrackers, whose loyalty and devotion are remarkable. And who would not give something to listen in at some ice cream shop in Balmain while the hero tells of his wonderful experiences of the day's play against the "big" bowlers? Young Jackson is going to wreck the averages of some bowlers. Fortunately, I'm in the same team, so it won't be mine.

The grade captains at Balmain were fighting over him by now, and it was felt by the seniors that the cries of "Too young!" by the lower grades were nothing more than a selfish attempt to keep the budding genius for themselves. When he was blooded in the first team in 1924-25, a season when Australia was in the fervid grip of another Ashes Test series (Arthur Mailey to the fore), Archie, at fifteen years and one month, was thought to be the youngest debutant ever in first-grade cricket.

He had been batting with such style and ease in fourth, third, and second grades that crowds were drawing away from the senior matches to see him—a diminutive performer whose pads flapped halfway up his thighs and whose flagging strength as the innings wore on found compensation in pliant wristwork, dancing feet, and uncanny timing and placement. Spectators at Birchgrove, seeing him strain under the weight of a man's bat, once clubbed together to buy him a lighter Harrow-sized bat.

He lived for cricket. If the silent films at the local cinema were disappointing he would go home before the end and, standing on the dining-room table, practise his footwork against the sideboard mirror—an old C.B. Fry pastime.

One of Archie's problems was sleepwalking, especially, it was noted, during the cricket season. His father found it best to tie up the bedroom door handle to save his son from falling over the lace ironwork which encased the balcony. Earlier, before the risk had been realised, he had actually spent the hotter, steamier nights on that balcony, where a bed had been wedged. His somnambulations sometimes led him down to the kitchen late at night. He would slump into the rocking chair while his mother, who knew how to handle him, carried on with her ironing. After a few minutes of unreal conversation she would direct him back to bed, and light snoring soon came as an assurance that the wanderings were at an end for one more night.

Archie ("The Champ") and Bill ("The Count") enjoyed their schooldays and made the best of them, for they tended to end early in Balmain. Having passed his Qualifying Certificate at fourteen, Archie had gone to Rozelle School; but a year later he was a schoolboy no more. The family needed his financial help, and he was eager to pay his way.

Joining Jackson (no relation) & McDonald, he worked distractedly in the warehouse until cricket got the better of him. As his career developed and his absences became more frequent he was compelled to leave J&M, and soon found himself employed by Alan Kippax in his sports shop in Martin Place. This city business had got away to a very sound start in 1926 after the Australian selectors had surprisingly overlooked Kippax for the tour of England ("I felt like jumping off The Gap," he reflected many years later). Now, after inviting the boy to call in, he opened a bank account for him and put him to work.

Kippax was to have a profound influence on Jackson as his mentor and captain in New South Wales matches. He gave him quiet guidance, encouragement, and, as his employer, generous time to practise and to play during the week.

In accordance with the residential qualification rules, Kippax played for Waverley, Jackson for Balmain, on the other side of town. But the Fates had brought this golden pair together, and Victor Trumper's ghost must have smiled.

Another benefactor had been Herbert Vere Evatt, then a young lawyer living in Balmain, and later to become one of Australia's most distinguished men: Chief Justice of New South Wales, Leader of the Federal Parliamentary Labor Party, Cabinet Minister, and President of the United Nations Assembly. Dr Evatt and Arthur Mailey saw to it that poverty never prevented a Balmain boy from having cricket equipment and being a paid-up member of the club.

The debt to these men and to sportsmaster Jack Mitchell was never forgotten by a remarkable quintet of lads from Rozelle

School who all became first-class cricketers: Archie Jackson, Bill Hunt, Syd Hird, Dudley Seddon, and Dick Nutt.

In 1923-24 Archie had made three centuries for Rozelle, and his average of 69 made no allowance for several retirements. He was also an "exceedingly fine slip field, and useful change bowler" who claimed on one exhilarating occasion 6 for 1, including a hat-trick.

He and Bill enjoyed their greatest success against Auburn School, whom they dismissed for 7 (including four byes)— Jackson 4 for 2, Hunt 6 for 1. Syd Hird, who later lived in South Africa, remembered Archie taking 8 for 2: "Yours truly claimed the other two for two runs." Hird also recalled a "tour" up to the Hawkesbury River, when the little Balmain cricketers were greeted almost with disdain. So they batted until almost 500 was on the board, and Archie was one of the centurymakers. They then dismissed the locals for 11 and 13 (or thereabouts).

Every evening the gang played in Birchgrove Park, where a rule had to be introduced to stop Archie batting forever: compulsory retirement at 100. Consequently, Archie, upon reaching the nineties, would stonewall. The answer had to be—and was—strategic overthrows to see him to three figures.

At Birchgrove, where Archie had captained the team at the age of twelve, making four centuries and taking 8 for 12 and 7 for 11, another sportsmaster often predicted that he would be playing for Balmain first team at seventeen, New South Wales at eighteen, and Australia at nineteen. The forecast was bold, yet, as it happened, safe. He was playing for the State at seventeen.

It was the same sportsmaster Byrnes who had felt Archie's absence through illness so severely in a crucial school match that he had authorised the boys to call round and plead with Mrs Jackson to let her son play. He was allowed to bat with a runner, made a few runs, and the Premiership was won.

He could not stay away from the game. His team-mates could never accept his absence with equanimity. This characteristic impatience in later years was to hasten his death.

In his first season in Balmain 1sts, following a moderate start and reversion to the 2nds, he was brought up again in an emergency and secured his place for the rest of his years. He was showing a solid defence and command of every stroke even if he was able to exert modest physical power. His highest was a fighting 41 not out in two hours, and he finished second in the averages with 30.75. Importantly, he was now equally at home on turf pitches.

He had batted fearlessly against the fireballs of Jack Gregory and Jack Scott and the briskness of Sam Everett and Charlie Kelleway, and the conclusion was inescapable: the "babe" had an uncanny instinct for batting. His greatest gift was that his afferent nerve (eye to brain) and efferent nerve (brain to limb) were abnormally sharp, as they are in all top sportsmen.

Nor did he merely allow his skill to evolve only in match play. He practised at Birchgrove Oval from five o'clock till dusk and was back for more in the clear morning air at half-past-seven before setting off to work. He was simply cricket-mad.

He was a keen reader, not only of Edgar Wallace and travel tales, famous lives and boy's adventure, but of cricket books— particularly those recording the great England v Australia battles.

Most of his dreams must have been of the "big cricket" which everyone in the district was now predicting for him, though on one sleepwalk he was climbing up to place files on an hallucinatory shelf, thinking himself to be at the warehouse. His father grabbed him as he was about to topple over the balcony. That would have been that.

As the 1925-26 season opened he was just sixteen. At first he struggled, and there were those who began to wonder if the frail prodigy had been but a momentary deception of Nature. Then the runs came.

As chronicled by Balmain's historian Cliff Winning, opening against Western Suburbs, Archie carried his bat doggedly for 58 out of 103 on a dreadful surface and made 61 in the second innings. His 88 against University was dazzling. And his first century in first-grade cricket was recorded against St George, a club due the following season to enlist a promising young fellow (D. Bradman) from the country. After Jackson's beautiful 129 there was a collection among the onlookers for which he shyly expressed his gratitude. There was jubilation in his home suburb.

At the end of the season he stood impertinently atop the Balmain averages with the considerable aggregate of 670 runs at almost 40. He had taken another step up the ladder in being selected for New South Wales 2nd XI against Victoria, making a modest 25 and 30 while the senior side in Sydney were piling up 708 (Kippax—overcoming a supposed nervous disposition yet again—making 271 not out).

To top off the summer Archie Jackson escaped the hurly-burly of first-grade cricket at Easter when 20 Balmain players and supporters travelled to Goulburn in three cars. Still short of full stature, Jackson extricated himself from the vehicle and made 59 and 74, and stroked 35 against Kenmore.

Home life continued as full of affection and animation as ever, with the unchangeably Scots parents quietly proud of their budding champion of a son and the sisters competing for his company. Dad, a physical-fitness obsessive who had an incurable weakness for impromptu chin-ups in the kitchen, was incapable of noisy pride, yet no father was ever more proud of a son's progress. This was the boy who, at the age of two and a half, had attracted a crowd at a Scottish holiday resort when giving a display of his virtuosity with a football. When his audience showed its appreciation the infant had indignantly bawled: "I don't want your money!" (in what must have been a Scottish accent, soon to be Australianised).

The family never ceased using certain peculiarly Scottish expressions even after many years of Balmain life, though Archie, as he grew up, spoke with care and ever-improving manner. Remembering him in the age of television, his sisters "heard" him whenever English actors Michael Wilding or Roger Moore (*The Saint and James Bond*) uttered their lines.

His love of reading matured into an interest in writing, evidenced firstly in his personal letters and later in his newspaper articles. J.C.Davis, Australia's authoritative cricket journalist, felt he could have become a writer of some distinction when his playing days were past, and not necessarily only on cricket. Davis had first seen him batting when his fame was nothing more than local. A friend, having watched schoolboy Archie a few days previously, had urged Davis to cast an eye over a "young Trumper". They went to Balmain.

"He looks to be Victor reborn," said the friend.

Davis, mesmerised, was bound to agree.

Yet if Trumper's mantle became an impediment to him, Archie Jackson was never to show it.

CHAPTER THREE

The Blooding

Engalnd took the Ashes from Australia in 1926. In a famous match at The Oval, where the honours were spread chiefly among the ancient Wilfred Rhodes, the new hope Harold Larwood, and the masterly Jack Hobbs and Herbert Sutcliffe, England finally buried Australia's dominance after four post-war series.

If not in mourning, Australia entered a period of anxious contemplation as the household names departed one by one: Herby Collins turned to full-time bookmaking, Warren Bardsley went into a sort of retirement, Johnny Taylor, troubled by war injuries, concentrated on his dental practice, Arthur Richardson moved to what was then cricket obscurity in Western Australia, and, most regretted, the troubled Charlie Macartney, "the Governor-General", retired after one further home season.

With several of the Test tourists delaying their return to Australia for the 1926-27 season, eyes turned to the youngsters, and in the laudable Australian tradition the New South Wales selectors searched for good cricketers without concerning themselves too much with the degree of dampness behind the prospects' ears.

Archie Jackson, Balmain's pride, grasped his chance with a sensational start to the grade season. His 111 against St George took only two hours. Against Western Suburbs he scored 143, this time his effortless leg-side play catching public attention. It was noted that he had gone easy for three innings "on account of a slight attack of ill-health", but after the triumph against Wests he hit yet another century, 158 in better than even time against Mosman. His tally for the year, as observed by Cliff Winning, came to 870 runs at 87, including five hundreds.

There had been no surprise when he was selected to play against Queensland in Brisbane, a city of destiny for him. He had had to negotiate the ordeal of a trial match at Sydney under the probing gaze of the past masters. As the aspirants went through their paces there was much shaking of heads: "then a fresh-faced, almost wisp of a boy, stepped through the gate of a fateful click which is music to the reminiscent champions". Two charming cuts that beat deep third man caused an instant stillness over the ground, then there was a chatter and shifting in chairs that betokened recognition of perfect strokeplay. It was "the advent of a master".

He went on to 53 before he was called in. Each stroke—the persuasive leaning drive where the ball did its own work, the leg glance, soundless in its delicacy—"brought the joyous light to sparkle in the eyes of the veterans".

His debut match in first-class cricket was Queensland's first in Sheffield Shield competition, and, to the relief of many, they performed splendidly, failing by only a fretful eight runs to make 400 for victory. The three big men of Queensland cricket all stamped themselves on the match: Leo O'Connor, run out for 196 to end it, Cecil Thompson, 134 in the first innings, and Ron Oxenham, seven wickets.

Jackson, true to a disconcerting habit, failed in New South Wales's first innings, but compensated with a second effort of 86, run out. Skipper Kippax made a century in each innings by way of inspiration.

Archie's one identifiable fault continued to be an occasional failing outside the off stump. Like Kippax, he was prone to dab late and wilfully at the away-swinger. If it came off, this lazy and now almost obsolete stroke sent the ball careering past the ankles of helpless slips fielders and into the boundary before third man could do anything about it. If it failed it looked dismal. He often murmured, "Don't cut, Archie, don't cut!" during the early stages of his innings.

But the cries that the youngster should put more "hammer" into his strokes were in vain. It would have been against Nature. He had a confessed love for applying the greatest velocity to the ball with the minimum of effort.

The selectors, it is said, were certain of his greatness from the start, and he was never really on trial. Quite to the contrary: he was to be permanently in the side, short of a calamity.

In the return match with Queensland, at Sydney, New South Wales were salvaged in the first innings by a Macartney century, but two hundreds by O'Connor won the match for Queensland, who piled up 577 in their reply. That they were eventually set as many as 300 to win was due to some fine batting in the second innings by Norman Phillips, Alan Kippax (who now had four centuries in five innings), and Archie Jackson, who scored 100 delightful runs.

He added 100 for the fourth wicket with Kippax, and although the 36-year-old Queensland captain, Leo O'Connor, was carried shoulder-high from the field at the end and joy was boundless in the visitors' dressing-room, there was immense satisfaction around Sydney that "Second-Innings" Jackson had escalated speculation into achievement.

The climax of his century was nerve-racking. He was on 99 when last man Ray McNamee came in to face the final ball of an over. He survived, and Archie took strike, needing a tremblingly important single. Four times he drove off the meat of the bat—straight to fieldsmen who refused to fumble. Then, as the clock struck noon, he managed to push an off-drive through, and his feet skimmed on down the pitch to the far end as the shrill roar of the crowd rose almost as a national hymn. He had passed his novitiate, and at 17 years and 92 days he remains (as of 2019) the youngest Australian to score a first-class hundred.

Just before Christmas he travelled with New South Wales on the southern tour, which this time produced two matches which were truly extraordinary examples of Australian first-class cricket's capacity for the grotesque. At Adelaide, South Australia made 500, to which New South Wales replied with 341—Jackson 4. By the time New South Wales batted again

CRADLE DAYS: A Glasgow studio photo of Archie Jackson, aged about one year, with his mother Margaret Jackson.

SOLEMN: Young Archie didn't enjoy having his picture taken on primary school photo day. The Jackson household was full of love, but there was not much money to go around: Archie made do with one pair of pants for most of his boyhood.

'BOY JACKSON': In a studio portrait later reproduced in newspapers, cherubic Archie looks as wary as ever of the camera's gaze.

↑ **JACKSON SENIOR:** Archie's father Alex 'Sandy' Jackson, who at 41 made the voyage from Glasgow to seek a brighter future for his family. The rest of the clan followed 18 months later.

→↗ **HAPPY HOME:** Archie out the front of the Jackson home at 14 Ferdinand Street, Balmain (ABOVE, RIGHT), from whose balcony the young, sleep-walking Archie nearly met his demise. The house still stands today. At right, Archie poses with Peggie, one of the proud sisters who doted on the only boy of the bunch, and the most incident-prone member of the Jackson brood.

FUTURE STARS: By the time Archie (LEFT), pictured here with Syd Hird, graduated to the Rozelle School cricket team, he was showing early glimpses of the brilliance to come. He took his place in a side that contained three other future first-class cricketers—Hird, Dudley Seddon, and Archie's best friend Bill Hunt. Like Archie, Hunt would join the ranks of Test cricketers, but went wicketless in his sole outing against South Africa.

↑ **LITTLE MASTERS:** Archie Jackson (seated to the left of the trophy) captained this smartly-attired Birchgrove school cricket team. The Jackson family home was barely 100 yards from Birchgrove Park.

↑ **STOMPING GROUND:** Balmain's Birchgrove Oval (ABOVE) as it greeted Archie in the 1920s. So dominant was he among the gang who gathered at the oval, a rule was introduced to stop Archie batting past 100. Soon Arthur Mailey was writing prophetically: "Balmain has developed a young batsman who may take a big part in Australian cricket."

STRIDING AHEAD:
Aged 17, with his sleeves rolled just clear of the wrists, and wearing the slatted pads of the era, the easy swing of Archie Jackson's bat shows he's now rather more than a twiglet of a batsman.

THE BIG TIME: The ease of style is apparent even from a distance. Jackson, opening the NSW innings with Jack Gregory against Victoria at Sydney in January 1928, plays fast bowler Frank Morton back down the pitch. This time the teenage batsman missed out, though a record eight centuries were scored in the match, four in this innings.

MAKING HIS WAY: An early team photo with Archie (THIRD FROM LEFT, STANDING) in a NSW side captained by Alan Kippax (FRONT ROW, THIRD FROM LEFT), another of the great batting stylists of the era, and featuring Archie's early backer, the Test spinner Arthur Mailey (FAR LEFT, SEATED).

SLIM CHAMPION: With the peak of his cap tucked down to shield the eyes, and his collar turned up for fielding duties, Archie Jackson surveys another field of glory.

Archie Jackson (signature)

BAGGY GREEN: Capped for the first time by his country during the 1928-29 Ashes series, Archie posed for this photograph taken by England's great batsman, Jack Hobbs. Both men were among the runs in Archie's debut Test. Hobbs opened the first innings with 74 runs for the tourists and Archie followed with the most memorable of debut centuries. At the end of a valiant chase of their 349-run fourth innings target, the home side fell 12 runs short. With that, England were 4-0 in the series.

↓ **BRAVE CLASSIC:** Adelaide, February 3, 1929, the end of an epic innings: A.A. Jackson lbw White 164. The 19-year-old's years of promise had crystalised into a brilliant innings on his Test debut against England.

↑ **LINEAGE:** The former Australian captain M.A. 'Monty' Noble instructs Archie (ABOVE, CENTRE) and teammates. Soon Jackson would join Noble in the ranks of Test cricketers, news in which Archie's parents Sandy and Margaret (ABOVE, RIGHT) delighted. Noble would dub Archie's debut 164 in the Adelaide Ashes Test of 1929 the "greatest knock of the series".

→ **HISTORY BOYS:** Archie takes a few pointers from Charles Bannerman, the man who faced Test cricket's first delivery in 1877, scored its first run, and stroked its maiden century. On his own Test debut, Archie would fall one short of Bannerman's totemic mark of 165.

↑ **DEBUT:** Having started with a majestic cover drive against Harold Larwood, Archie eased into his maiden Test innings with this stroke off England's left-arm spinner, Jack White.

↑ **DREAM START:** The Adelaide Oval scoreboard displaying Archie's magnificent century on Test debut against England.

FULL FLIGHT: Pounding the off-side field; some of Jackson's cuts and drives during his glorious innings of 182 in the Test Trial at Sydney in December, 1929.

← **EARLY GLIMPSES:** The supple elegance of the young Archie Jackson is evident in this crisp drive off the bowling of Queensland's Ron Oxenham, the all-rounder whose second Test appearance was the 1929 Adelaide Test in which Archie made his debut.

they needed an astronomical 446 for victory.

They made them. T.J. E. "Tosser" Andrews hit 126, Phillips 52, Kippax 42; but the vital contributions came from Morgan (116) and Jackson (56 not out). They added 130 for the sixth wicket, and with 20-year-old Jim Hogg as his seventh-wicket partner, Jackson tapped Arthur Richardson through mid-on and scampered the winning run.

It had been the most significant two hours he had yet spent at the wicket, and as he waited for his partner to join him and support him through the embarrassment of the return to their jubilant team-mates, he might well have reflected that the victory was all the more praiseworthy for having been achieved against two very fine spinners: Arthur Richardson and Clarrie Grimmett, who had secured only one wicket apiece in 64 overs.

The excitement was short-lived. At Melbourne, after being dismissed for 221, they fielded, eagerly and tirelessly, for ten and a half hours while Victoria amassed a world record 1107 runs. Bill Ponsford (352) narrowly missed Clem Hill's record 365 not out, bemoaning his "bad luck" when he finally played on. An unprecedented 573 runs were hit on the second day; Hendry (100) and Ryder (295) both, according to the former, hitting with gay abandon in the half-hope of being caught, but succeeding only in hitting huge fours and sixes. Andy Ratcliffe, undeterred by a couple of costly errors, kept wicket keenly throughout; and Arthur Mailey's characteristic summary became a national joke: "It was rather a pity Ellis got run out at 1107 because I was just striking a length. Very few chances were given, but I think a chap in a tweed coat dropped Jack Ryder near the shilling stand!"

Mailey took 4 for 362 off 64 eight-ball overs, all bowled into the wind. His stoicism and tactical conviction were seen as misguided by some. If he had bowled with the wind, they said, he would have placed the onus on the batsmen hitting against it.

Fifty thousand cheered the thousand up and the passing of the previous world record of 1059—both events carried by the ebullient Jack Ellis, who bellowed "Long live Victoria!" as he bolted the vital runs.

Archie Jackson, having made 4 in the first innings and run himself ragged in the field, dredged up the stamina to score an unbeaten 59 as New South Wales subsided to 230 all out. "Glad to have seen it all," was the general summary among spectators, "but not again. Bad for cricket."

On New Year's Day, Jackson played for E. L.Waddy's team against Northern Tasmania, a match at Launceston which was not of first-class status. This time it was the turn of the New South Welshmen to make and not chase runs. Kippax made 132, Waddy 112, Sullivan 124, and Jackson 160.

An official approached Kippax during the tea interval and asked if he and Jackson, who was still batting with him, might help the scorers to differentiate between them, so similar did they appear in the middle. Could one of the batsmen possibly wear a coloured waist sash? It would look rather absurd, thought Kippax, but yes, of course, they would co-operate: Archie would wear the sash.

A week later, back on the mainland, Jackson made his first duck in big cricket, caught behind. South Australia piled on the runs in their second innings, diminutive Karl Schneider's 146 remarkably containing only three fours, and New South Wales found themselves needing 547 for victory. They had made 446 to win the Adelaide match. What was an extra hundred runs?

But there was to be no second miracle. "Perker" Lee's off-breaks accounted for 5 for 36, and the visitors won by more than 300 runs. New South Wales's measly 206 owed much to the trusty Kippax, who made 52 . . . and even more to his seventeen-year-old protégé, 104 not out.

The score had been 37 for 4 when Jackson went in. Tearaway Jack Scott was bowling with rare devil and the wily Grimmett was wheeling away. In the face of this, Jackson stroked 50 in even time, and his century partnership with Kippax came in only 71 minutes. The fledgling then hedged, creeping unsteadily to 97 before sliding a beautiful drive through the covers for two. Then there was an overthrow and he had his first century on the Sydney Cricket Ground. Fieldsmen shared his thrill and ran to congratulate him. Nearly a century later this still gives Archie Jackson the great distinction of first place and second among the youngest Australian first-class century-makers.

A.R.B. "Pedlar" Palmer, sports editor of Sydney's *Daily Guardian*, was struck by Archie's classical style during this innings, noting how deceptive was his reach: "He steps forward to cover-drive—not far enough is one's first impression; he'll lift that ball—but his wrists come into play, and the stroke is perfectly balanced and true . . . the bat seems to be a whip in his hands."

Now he had absolutely no chance of escaping the brand of "second-innings batsman". In five matches he had made

| 39 |

17 runs in the first innings and 405 (for twice out) in the second.

It was time for another sensation, and once more Victoria provided it. Coming to Sydney without Ponsford, Woodfull or Ryder, far from making a thousand runs, they were cast aside by Ray McNamee and Charlie Macartney for 35. The pitch was no fun to bat on, even if it had been when New South Wales started the match: Kippax batted for less than four hours for his 217.

This was Macartney's final Sheffield Shield appearance, although a month later he took a more remunerative final bow at Sydney in a benefit match played between the 1926 Australian XI and The Rest. Kippax, who had been omitted from that touring team, made a hundred against the Test team that for personal and obvious reasons gave him intense satisfaction. And in the second innings, on his way to 51, he passed a thousand runs for the season.

The Australian XI made 533, Woodfull and Andrews getting hundreds and Ponsford registering his sixth in successive matches. But for all the cascade of runs, it was universally accepted that Jackson's 32 in the next innings was the most attractive innings of all. He eventually fell to his old Balmain tutor and mentor, Arthur Mailey, caught-and-bowled. There was some doubt about the catch, and Mailey frowned tentatively towards the umpire. However, when he turned around, Jackson had gone, satisfied he was out.

In first-class cricket Archie Jackson had made 500 runs at an average of 50, and in spite of having missed several grade matches he finished with 870 runs for Balmain, scoring, in

12 innings, five centuries and a 96 (which included a rare six onto the embankment). This total put him at the top of the Sydney grade aggregates—the first Balmain player ever to take that honour. His rich tally stood as a club record for 53 years, until Englishman Mike Gatting made 878 (in many more —19—innings) in the 1979-80 season. And because he had played first-class cricket, Archie was not permitted to play for Balmain's Under-21 Poidevin-Gray team. In all matches this season he fashioned 1716 runs at 78.

Jackson had been an object of fascination to the great as well as the humble onlookers. Clem Hill identified him as the great discovery, "the biggest find since Ponsford". He liked Archie's sparkling footwork, his movement in the field, reminiscent of Johnny Taylor. He had watched him closely enough even to notice that his toes turned in slightly as he walked.

Another of his idiosyncrasies was the wearing of his sleeves almost down to the wrists. What very few people knew was that this was not in imitation of Kippax nor solely to prevent sunburn on his Celtic skin. He was troubled by psoriasis, a skin inflammation which stems from a faulty immune system and for which there was then no known cure. Archie Jackson was oppressively conscious of the small, flaky, crusty, silver-red patches on his back and arms. So well did he conceal the problem that the majority of his team-mates remained unaware. Frank Buckle, a fine batsman early in the century and later manager of a New South Wales side that included Archie, recalled how he would endeavour to shower privately at the end of play, and often left a trail of talcum powder in his wake.

That dour batsman Charlie Kelleway, in assessing the

exciting new youngster, was guarded, even critical. He disliked the flourish, especially in his back play, when the bat often came down fractionally late. He wished he would not be so "cramped with copying other batsmen's styles. These might be above or even below his standard." The summary came as a comfort: "These flaws are only trifles and, therefore, easily rectified, but need to be pointed out by the right person."

Alan Kippax, one suspects, was not everywhere considered to be the right person. Yet Archie Jackson, being a child of Nature like Denis Compton later and Ricky Ponting later still, simply had to bat in a certain manner and no other.

Jackson had absorbed the advice of many along the line: George Blakemore at Birchgrove School, Jack Mitchell at Rozelle School, Arthur Mailey, with his insight and good humour, and Jimmy Searle at the SCG nets—Searle, who gave his heart and soul to his Colts years after suffering the unenvied and probably unique distinction of having shattered a bone in his leg in colliding with the gutter while fielding at the Sydney Cricket Ground back in 1889.

But of them all it was the example of Alan Kippax, ever near, that had the greatest effect. So uncannily similar were they that A.B.R. Roche, a grazier from Goodooga who befriended Archie and led him into the world of literature, art and the theatre, was moved to write (perhaps arguing the point unto himself) a personal analysis of the two most absorbing batting styles to be seen in Australia between the two wars:

Alan, after he took block, shuffled forward in front of the wicket a fraction of an inch at a time till the ball was delivered. Archie never moved. Archie in his forward driving strokes used his whole body from toes to head, and he only straightened up after contact. His leg glance and square cut and late cut were altogether his own. Heard Bradman once say "How do you manage that leg glance?" The answer was: "I don't know." All his strokes were natural and his only. He never did Kippax's chop. You ask any Queensland cricketer.

CHAPTER FOUR

To New Zealand

He was eighteen at the start of the 1927-28 season, and had there been a Test series almost certainly he would have taken part in it. As it was, he had a sniff of international cricket early in the season in the match between New South Wales and the homecoming New Zealanders, who had recently surprised England with their batting strength. That their bowling lacked penetration was revealed by the State side as they accumulated 571. Jack Gregory smashed a century before lunch and added 262 with Tommy Andrews in two dazzling hours: real T20 stuff before its time. Later Kippax and Jackson stroked a century stand in the astonishing time of 36 minutes and were not separated until they had put together 176. Each made a century (Archie's coming in a mere 71 minutes) and New South Wales won by 10 wickets.

Jackson was now a Balmain selector with Arthur Mailey and

George Wheatley, picking many a young player—though he relinquished the responsibility halfway through this summer because of his New South Wales playing responsibilities. He was quickly into his stride. This swift hundred against the Kiwis followed an innings of 108 against Wauchope during a country tour with Kippax's side, and he also hit a two-hour century off North Sydney, for whom Bill O'Reilly had just come up from the country to enlist. It was one of the uncommon occasions when "Tiger" failed to take a wicket. A second grade hundred came off Western Suburbs.

In November, Jackson accompanied the New South Wales team to Brisbane and was among the early calamities as his side lost four for 17. There was no play on the second and third days, and though the visitors had to follow on, there was no time for Queensland to force outright victory.

A fortnight later he was again eased out of the picture, firstly by a boil on the knee, then by two early dismissals against Victoria. The knee became troublesome during the journey across the continent, and his withdrawal from the South Australia match allowed young Don Bradman to make his first-class debut. He scored 118.

In Melbourne the stumbling block was the ubiquitous Ponsford who, having started the season with 133 and a world record 437, now made 202 (and was to follow it with 336 in the next match), thus having broken the heart of every Sheffield Shield bowler in the land. The aged Ironmonger and Blackie (both 45) finished the job when New South Wales batted, though McNamee had stolen some of the glory for the vanquished by taking 7 for 77. The match was further notable for Woodfull (with his own score 191) making the first second-innings declaration in the history of the competition.

Home in Sydney, Jackson remained in the doldrums during the New Year match with Queensland. It was a remarkable contest, Kippax scoring 315 not out and later enforcing the follow-on. So well did Queensland bat this time that when New South Wales tried for the 227 for victory they were hard put to stave off defeat: Otto Nothling used a rain-damaged pitch to advantage and had 5 for 39 when time ran out.

Next day New South Wales went straight into the return with South Australia, and if Archie Jackson was anxious and impatient for a return to form, he kept it to himself. Bill Hunt recalled how, on the infrequent occasions when Archie lifted a ball around that time, it seemed to go to hand. But he was never one for making excuses.

"What did that one do, Archie?" invariably brought a stock reply: "Got a good'un!"

Any good'uns he received in this South Australia match he dealt with ably enough—in both innings. Kippax decided he should open, rather than sit watching his companions make runs while he died a thousand deaths. He made 131 and 122, and returned to the headlines with a smiling vengeance.

The first innings took four hours, the second an hour less; and once more the Sydney crowd were treated to a Jackson-Kippax stand of charm and substance as they added 132 at a crucial stage of the second innings. The pitch had been deadened by rain, and yet Jack Scott (playing his nineteenth season) and Tim Wall needed watching. Scott erred in one over by bowling so wide and short that Jackson ignored the lot, but the tactics might have been deliberate for the batsman showed every sign of "nibbling", perhaps in his anxiety to keep the scoreboard rolling now that he was through the nervous beginnings. His local followers, spread across the Hill and sitting intently in the Members' Stand, were not at all appreciative of the heart spasms he gave them at regular intervals.

One report of the match grumbled that after an hour's play New South Wales had made "only" 51. But though Jackson was in for over an hour and a half before hitting his second four, he kept the singles coming.

The third prong of the attack was Clarrie Grimmett, dropping the ball as if radar-guided onto a teasing spot from a trajectory so flat that even the fleetest-footed batsman was tested almost beyond endurance. Jackson handled him well throughout—even plundered him once in a while: one soaring off-drive cleared the fence. He played cat and mouse with Vic Richardson's field-setting, drawing the cover men in, driving them out, and piercing the arc with marvellous precision. The only major hitch in his first innings was an unpleasant blow to the groin from Tim Wall. For some time he hobbled about in agony.

The ground was hushed as he reached 99 in the second innings. Scott hurtled in, bowled, and Jackson turned him for a single that made him the youngest batsman ever to record two separate hundreds in a first-class match.

The 16,000 cheered, whistled and clapped before filtering home, their day handsomely made. Among them were Archie's mother and father—Mrs Jackson, usually tied to the home, having watched only one cricket match before in her entire life. Their pride was immeasurable long before Archie brought home the silver plate presented by the New South Wales Cricket Association.

When Victoria came to Sydney there were batfuls of runs to be had, but the ironic fact was that Jackson (11 and 44) missed out, Ponsford (6 and 2), perhaps dried up from previous efforts, missed out, Jack Gregory, with whom Jackson opened the New South Wales innings, missed out, and, in the first innings, so did Bradman. But eight centuries were scored in front of a record crowd. In this initial season of time-limit matches the batsmen had continued to hold sway.

Archie Jackson, as this match ground its way to a draw, was called upon to bowl and conceded 13 runs in three overs without taking a wicket, an apt return for a ninth-change who, nevertheless, continued to regard himself as a bowler of some potential.

The remainder of the season was swallowed up by a tour of New Zealand with an Australian side composed of some established cricketers and some of the promising youngsters (although Bradman was left at home as a possible replacement). Among the hopefuls were W.C. (Colin) Alexander and Karl Schneider from South Australia, and Jackson and McNamee from New South Wales, but none of them was to reach or remain at the pinnacle of the game for long. Two faded from big cricket and two died young.

The first signs of Schneider's fatal illness showed on this tour. At a mere 5 ft 2 ins and easily the smallest first-class cricketer in Australia, this left-hand opening batsman had shown remarkable skill during his youth in Melbourne. Removing to

Adelaide, he soon made his mark, even with the handicaps of a short reach and an absence of power in his shots. England Test batsman Patsy Hendren, then coaching in Adelaide and indulging in the fashionable odium of comparisons, saw him as "the coming Warren Bardsley".

Schneider made over 500 runs in New Zealand, but towards the end of the tour he collapsed while on picnic with the team on the slopes of Mount Cook. Several of them were out riding when he suffered a haemorrhage. Among those who carried him back to the hut was Archie Jackson, whose family were never able to erase the query from their minds: was this a dangerous point of contact? But Karl Schneider died from leukemia, not tuberculosis, six months later, on September 5, 1928, which happened to be Archie Jackson's nineteenth birthday; he was just 23.

The tour had started brightly enough. Jackson and W.C. "Billy" Bull, the manager, both from the Balmain club, were given a rousing send-off at a dinner at the Dungowan Café. Archie, now a member of the General Committee, though his attendances dropped away steadily over the three seasons he served until his withdrawal in 1930, listened to his skipper, George Wheatley, recall the lad's wonderful 158 against Mosman. Hal Hooker had been swinging the ball two feet that afternoon, but Jackson was master. When he came back into the pavilion it was "with extreme modesty and the air of having accomplished nothing at all".

Bull responded for the guests of honour with greater ease than the sweaty-palmed Jackson, who was incurably uneasy on such occasions, though he expressed gratitude at the presentation travelling bag which the club members hoped would serve him through many a tour.

The Australians in New Zealand were unbeaten—in fact untroubled. Woodfull and Ponsford made runs galore and Grimmett, feted as a returning hero wherever he went in this land of his birth, took 74 wickets, twice as many as Don Blackie, next highest.

Jackson began with 72 against Nelson, 44 against North Otago, and 63 against Otago, then compiled a stylish 110 at Invercargill against Southland, putting on 220 for the first wicket with Bill Ponsford, who also made 110—a score that irritated him because he seemed to make it so often (in his first Test match, too).

The tour was also a social success, though *Smith's Weekly* recorded that Archie was so much in demand, especially by the two daughters of a prominent King's Counsel, that the only ploy guaranteed to overcome his shyness was to invite manager Bull to their father's home. The young cricketer invariably accompanied him.

By the time the party reached Gisborne for the eleventh match Archie was mentally and physically weary. In a letter to Bill Hunt he confessed the fact, and also told of a hair-raising incident down in the caves:

> We have been having a great time over here, although I am heartily sick of cricket, and only wish now that we were down at Mt Cook for a good rest. I had a funny experience last week. After we left New Plymouth we spent two hours at the Waitomo Caves, which are amongst the most beautiful in the world. However, just as we were leaving we decided to go down in the boat and view the glow-worms, which at this time

were shining beautifully.

Anyway, as I was getting out I fell in the water amid a hell of a row and got a bit of a ducking. There were quite a number as wet as me, because when I got back into the boat I walked over everyone! But it was certainly funny while it lasted.

Clarrie Grimmett remembered the incident vividly 44 years later: "Archie was in the bow, and as we approached the landing he tried to pull the boat in, but instead, pushed it away and fell into the black muddy water. Pandemonium broke out as he couldn't swim and we couldn't see him in the darkness. Eventually we got him out, and when we saw him in the light he was absolutely covered in black mud. We took him back to the hotel, washed his clothes, and as we were due to go on to our next town we hung his clothes out of the train windows to dry them and put a rug around him."

It was a huge joke to Archie, who concluded his letter to Bill Hunt:

I suppose I had better close now as we are going out to a party, but I hope you get among the runs and wickets before the season ends. Hoping to hear from you soon.

Your very sincere pal,
Archie Jackson

Hunt was gradually making his mark as a versatile and aggressive slow-medium left-arm bowler who played and expostulated in a manner that sometimes provoked opponents—and, in some cases, his own team-mates. No respecter of persons, Bill trod on toes, laughed infectiously, paid the price occasionally, and would never have changed a minute of it when it came time to look back. From the New South Wales ranks he was eventually chosen to play for Australia against South Africa at Adelaide in the 1931-32 series. Archie's health had given way by then, and his pleasure and expressions of congratulation had the edge taken off them by a mutual regret that the Balmain boys were not wearing Australia's colours alongside each other.

Bill did the next-best thing. He wore Archie's flannels, in spite of an observable tightness. He could never explain quite what made him do it. As it happened, it was his one fond memory of his only Test match. He made 0, took no wickets, and held a solitary catch. Worse, he had a serious difference with the captain, W.M. Woodfull, who was horrified by some of Bill's language, and a year later he was finding his happiness in the Lancashire League with Rishton.

Archie, able to speak as a very close friend, blamed Bill for the breach: "I know both of you well enough and I understand both of you. You should have given way, Bill." It was a simple analysis, and certainly near the mark.

For his part, Bill, whose great-heartedness was often masked by a boisterous exuberance, gave his only son two of the most evocative names in cricket: Alan Archie.

The New Zealand tour was wound up with two matches against representative XIs. Jackson, playing in only the first, at Auckland, was caught-and-bowled for 35 by the talented leg-spinner Billy Merritt, and the match was drawn. Woodfull made 284 and featured in two long stands: 184 with Ponsford and 218 with the ill-fated Schneider.

Archie wrote again after that match, and showed his customary concern for his club's affairs:

Balmain seems to have fared very badly, but I heard that some of you were batting against Jack Gregory in the dark, which I don't suppose is too good a feeling, eh?

Next Saturday the last match of the tour starts, and I will be very pleased indeed when I can say goodbye to my cricket togs for another 6 months anyway.

George Wheatley got out of his trouble all right? Those newspaper reporters make a hell of a row about nothing. They're always the same—always hanging about the dressing-room and when anything happens never forget to put the boot in.

Well, Bill, I suppose I must close now, but I won't be sorry when we're on the Tahiti on our way back to Sydney.

Only a few months earlier that same Union Steamship Tahiti had been in a collision with a ferry in Sydney Harbour. Forty people, including many schoolchildren, were killed. In 1930 the sorry vessel herself sank off New Zealand.

CHAPTER FIVE

Glory at Adelaide

Percy Chapman's 1928-29 MCC team achieved just about as much success as any England side could ever reasonably expect on a tour of Australia. Winning four of the Tests and losing the fifth, outclassing the States until the fatigued later stages, and boasting a front rank of Hammond, Hobbs, Sutcliffe, Hendren, Jardine, Larwood, Tate, White and Geary, they were truly what they styled themselves on the Christmas cards they sent home: "A Happy Family in Australia".

Australia, for its part, starting with an over-mature side which was soon diminished by the enforced withdrawal of Jack Gregory and Charles Kelleway, could look back at the end of the rubber upon the successful initiation of only two youngsters: Don Bradman and Archie Jackson. But what youngsters.

The first Test, in which Bradman made his debut, was catastrophic for Australia. Chapman, with a first-innings lead of 399, declined to apply the follow-on and Australia, eventually set 742 for victory, with Gregory and Kelleway unfit, rotted away on a dampened Brisbane Exhibition Ground surface for 66.

Bradman was dropped, but when Ponsford's hand was broken by Larwood in the second Test, which England took by eight wickets, Bradman found himself reinstated for the third Test, which England won by a much narrower margin. He made 79 and 112, and not only established his place in the side, but became the centrepiece of world cricket for the next twenty years.

It was not until the fourth Test, at Adelaide, that room could be found for Archie Jackson. The public clamour for his selection had been persistent, and as Australia so desperately needed somebody to support Woodfull at the opening of the innings, this was the supreme opportunity for inducting the most golden of hopes.

It had to be at the expense of Vic Richardson, whose 82 for South Australia against the Englishmen just before the Test was made off a Larwoodless attack. After learning of his omission, Richardson promptly signed up to give the first live Test cricket broadcast from Adelaide Oval.

Richardson's only remaining claim to inclusion—after four batting failures—might have been his sterling fielding. Here Jackson had a curious reputation. His attention still seemed often to wander, and the lethargy which observers found excusable and even admirable in his batting brought forth unfavourable comment in the outfield. When moved to it, he could swoop on an apparent boundary hit and have it back to the wicketkeeper almost as fast as any. Perhaps it was the poet in him that misted up his concentration.

If he had made a lot of runs in the Test Trial at Melbourne at the start of the season the series might well have run a straighter course for Australia. But he hadn't. The only bright performance by an untried player in the Trial was Queenslander Ron Oxenham's 10 wickets, and it was not until the third Test that he was awarded a baggy green cap. Jackson had shaped competently, particularly against the pace of Jack Gregory. But he did not make enough runs.

He did well for New South Wales in Brisbane, where they needed 399 to win, and made them comfortably. In the first innings he added 113 with Bradman, who scored a century in each innings, and in the thrilling final assault he and Roy Loder posted 121 for the first wicket.

Then Archie Jackson faced English bowling for the first time—after fielding to a declared total of 734 which was nothing less than a glorious exhibition of masterly English batsmanship. Walter Hammond, who made 225 on this favourite Sydney ground, added a record 333 with Patsy Hendren, who was in a hard-hitting mood despite (or perhaps because of) a gale-force wind that blew his cap off. Douglas Jardine also made a classic century, it was something for the studious youngster to digest.

Maurice ("Chub") Tate beat Jackson with pace and bowled him for only 4, and New South Wales in due course had to follow on. This time he got a start. Morgan and Andrews were dismissed, but Jackson, in company with Kippax, seemed able to handle the situation. It was his first taste of Harold Larwood's furious pace, but when he was 40, and the innings was warming, he embarked on a run, misconstruing Kippax's follow-through off a stroke to "Tich" Freeman, then hesitated. By then Kippax had responded, and would have been stranded. Jackson, never one to shirk obligation, walked past his captain and became the victim of Jardine's underarm throw. The sacrifice paid handsomely, for Kippax and the next man in, Bradman, saved the match with unbeaten centuries. And both were selected for the first Test.

There was one further chance before the Australian team was chosen, and that was several days later when an Australian XI (without any Victorians) played the touring MCC at Sydney. This time Larwood won the first bout, having Jackson caught wide at slip off a weak dab. But in the second innings, again going in at No.4, he began confidently and batted as his supporters would have wished.

He was graceful, if not commanding. He was never willing or able to collar an attack brutally, excitedly or arrogantly. To those who preferred batting of that kind, he never did quite measure up. These were the folk who played Wagner recordings loudly on their wind-up gramophones. Jackson fans preferred something much lighter and beguiling.

So, having made a noteworthy 61 before glancing a difficult catch to Duckworth, he may well have nurtured private hopes of inclusion in the Test team. But he had to wait a while yet. It could not be a bad thing for someone only nineteen years old.

A month passed before his next big match. This was the Sheffield Shield contest with Victoria at Melbourne over Christmas, and an historic and bizarre match it was. Victoria made 376, which seemed more than ample as New South Wales collapsed to 113 for 9 (Jackson 19 after opening with his hefty friend, Alan "Noodles" Fairfax). However, Alan Kippax and Hal Hooker added a hundred runs for the last wicket, and then another hundred, and then yet another, to create a world record which must surely be eternal: 307 for the tenth wicket. Kippax finished 260 not out and No.11 Hooker was finally caught for 62.

The New Year match against Queensland found the northern State again a formidable proposition. Cec Thompson governed affairs with over 200 runs and six wickets, and when Jackson batted a second time, for 53 not out, he had to defend grimly for the sake of his side.

He needed something a little more spectacular than that, and not for the first time South Australia were the punchbag. The setting was Adelaide, and Jackson came within an ace of repeating his feat against them at Sydney the previous season of a century in each innings. Crafty spinner Grimmett and fast man Wall provided the obstacles, and the young man, in company with his captain, danced his way across them all. His 162 took slightly less than five hours, two hours of which were spent adding 221 with Kippax.

Archie Jackson sometimes found difficulty in piercing the field, especially when he was on 99. It was galling. Then he tucked the ball away through slips to reach his century, and instantly accelerated, taking another 50 runs in as many minutes. When Fairfax was in obvious bother against Grimmett, Jackson kept him away from the strike until he himself was bowled by the crafty little spinner.

New South Wales fell away alarmingly in the second innings, and this time Jackson found support in "Cassie" Andrews, who made 87. Then, with only 10 needed for his second hundred of the match (it would have been his fifth in a row against South Australia), gallingly Jackson was caught.

"Jackson for Australia!" went up the cry once more from a public agitated at seeing their Test team now three-down in the 1928-29 series, with two to play. The Ashes were now lost, but perhaps there might yet be kindled some hope for the future.

Victoria came to Sydney, and New South Wales hit 713 for 6 off them. Jackson made 41, Fairfax 104, but the glory belonged to D. G. Bradman, whose 340 not out broke a number of old and revered records. This small, alert man had stamina, and he could never be persuaded to agree that he had made enough runs. Old "Dainty" Ironmonger knew this, having taken 2 for 220 off 56 overs. Herb Gamble thought so too: he had 2 for 193 off 29 overs. And the Victoria fast-medium bowler Hans Ebeling hadn't even a success to cherish in 39 eight-ball overs.

How they must have envied Hal Hooker who, having made his mark as a No.11 batsman a month earlier, polished off the Victoria innings with a hat-trick and took a wicket with his first ball in their follow-on innings to make it four in four. Victoria passed 500 this time, but the first-innings points gave New South Wales the Sheffield Shield for the only time during Archie Jackson's playing career.

By now he was the centre of attention, for the big moment

had arrived: he had been invited to play for Australia in the fourth Test, at Adelaide, starting on February 1, 1929. Arthur Mailey scuttled over from *The Sun* newspaper offices and gave the glad tidings to Archie, his former ward. Balmain buzzed with joy and pride.

Extraordinarily, England, in the last Test played at Adelaide four years previously, had lost a high-scoring match by the slender margin of 11 runs, and this time the result was to be just as razor-thin.

There were several heroes in the match, but three men towered from it: for England, Walter Hammond, who made 119 not out and 177 (following Test scores of 251, 200 and 32), and Jack White, the Somerset slow left-arm bowler (and farmer) who appeared such an easy proposition to the distant spectator, and yet, with his coiling wrist action, made the ball dip late in flight and often deviate in towards the batsman. Bowling off a short approach, he had by now destroyed all Australian hopes that he would tire sooner or later. In this match he floated down 60 six-ball overs in the first innings and 64.5 in the second, taking 5 for 130 and 8 for 126. ("I used a few shirts and several whisky-and-sodas," he said.)

For Australia the demi-god was the new opening batsman, A.Jackson—soon to be known as A.A.Jackson when he decided to insert his father's name, Alexander, as much in pride as to add uniformity to a scorecard wherein everyone else boasted two initials.

It was very hot as England batted first, and Hobbs and Sutcliffe monumentally raised 143 for the first wicket. Soon, however, the side was in mild difficulties against Australia's spinners, and it was left to Hammond in one of the toughest innings of his life to carry them to 334. Grimmett bowled craftily, and with due reward took 5 for 102. Surprisingly he bowled a wide, a phenomenon in such a parsimonious bowler.

Then, in mid-afternoon on the Saturday, Bill Woodfull and Archie Jackson went to the middle to answer for Australia (Jackson having sustained a mild thigh strain while fielding). Some felt that the youngster was being thrown in at the deep end when Ryder cast him as an opener, but class usually carries the day. Many were the prayers that the slim young man's first-innings hoodoo would not strike in this particular match.

Within minutes the anxiety was directed to the other end: Woodfull was cleverly caught down the leg side by George Duckworth for 1; Hunter "Stork" Hendry, on 2, nibbled at Larwood and was also held by the keeper; and Kippax (3) was yorked by White, who had been brought on for a couple of overs to enable Larwood and Tate to change ends.

Thus Australia were in a state of shock with three down for 19. The only cheer for the onlookers had come from the unworried manner of "Boy" Jackson. He drove Maurice Tate handsomely and put the full face of the bat to the high pace of Larwood. Whenever Tate pitched on or just outside leg stump Jackson flicked him away through square leg. In this worsening crisis it brought lumps to the throats of the tense onlookers.

Umpire George Hele, writing later of his close-up view of the Test match newcomer, explained that the spectators were being deluded by the distant, young, faceless figure standing up to the English onslaught. Archie had leaned forward to his first ball from Tate, who appealed for lbw before noticing that the ball had gone for four. "This kid'll get a century" murmured the burly, jolly bowler. Hele recalled the moment of crisis:

> I stole a glance at him. An umpire is not supposed to have any feelings, but I was just as keenly interested to see Jackson succeed as any of the 50,000 spectators. It was with something like dismay that I saw Jackson standing there with his face as white as a sheet and nervously trying to moisten his lips. Anybody would have felt sympathetic towards Jackson if they had caught the glimpse I had of him. What a position to be in!

It was not the position for long. Australia's captain Jack Ryder came in at No.5, and his immediate willingness to play shots served as a reminder that in the Adelaide Test four years ago he had made 201 not out. Now he was driving Larwood with rare severity. "Stick to it, son," he kept saying to Archie between overs. "You'll be all right, son."

Jackson saw a ball well pitched up from White, stepped forward, waited for a split second, and whipped it through the covers to raise the 50. Ryder caught up with him at 30, but he went ahead again and the cheering was tumultuous when he reached his personal 50. The Englishmen were recognising that a rare talent had entered Test cricket. They too showed their appreciation, wondering, perhaps, what awaited them in the long run, with Bradman already in Australia's high ranks.

It took Ryder and Jackson only 105 minutes to add 100 runs out of the tense situation created by Kippax's dismissal. The skipper shortly reached his own 50, a sound performance, but quite overshadowed by his tousle-haired young partner, physically so far removed from the archetypal Aussie.

At the end of that sweltering day, with a Sunday of welcome

rest to follow, Australia were 131 for 3, Jackson 70, Ryder 54, still 293 behind. But Jackson's polished offering had recharged Australia's interest and renewed their faith. Heavy hearts had been lifted, and E.H.M.Baillie (*Sporting Globe*) was not the only onlooker to compare the youngster's beautiful batsmanship to that of the hallowed Victor Trumper: "He played all the bowlers with a confidence and a gracefulness that won the hearts of onlookers. His on-side play particularly was strong, but he made flashing drives and cover shots, and occasionally a delightful cut. In defence he was always well behind the ball with a perfectly straight bat, and many of his defensive shots were turned into run-getters by the wristiness of his play."

There had been only one false stroke—an intended glance off Larwood which sent the ball curling up off the edge of the bat just short of the 46-year-old Jack Hobbs in the covers. Otherwise Jackson's poise grew more apparent as the long session wore on. Tea had been taken between innings, and during this gruelling 160-minute period England's tireless seam bowler George Geary was forced to leave the field with a leg injury.

When he reached the sanctuary of the dressing-room Jackson was limp. "We had to mop him with cold towels," recalled "Stork" Hendry forty years later as he gazed sadly into space from a wicker chair on his verandah. He spoke his thoughts aloud, as if alone in a meadow: "Poor little devil."

Ryder had a tendency to get out early in the morning upon resuming a longish innings, and on the Monday it happened again. He attempted to pull-drive slow left-armer White, who was nagging away still on a perfect length with no-one out for the shot. Ryder was tempted, missed, and adjudged leg-before.

Australia suffered no further losses before lunch, though they needed luck. Bradman looked anything but secure, and Jackson, the talk of the nation now, was tight with tension at the thought of reaching a hundred that would place him in the very select band of those who had made a century in their first England-Australia Test innings. Not only had he the chance of joining that aristocracy, but he would become the youngest member. For today, February 4, 1929, he was just 19 years and 152 days old.

He had extended his score to 97 by lunch, having truly locked the gate: he had added a mere 27 runs in the 90 minutes of play. Just previously, a gorgeous late-cut off Geary took him into the nineties—a relief after numerous firm drives had been blocked off by White's cover fieldsmen, Hobbs commanding. Someone wrote more appropriately than he might have realised that throughout that hot, battling morning Jackson had played "Scotch". The two minors, Jackson and Bradman, had weathered tantalising slow bowling, with Larwood at the other end sometimes bowling to *a concentrated leg-side field of four between fine and square leg*, an eerie foreshadowing of the dreaded Bodyline which was to come four years later, though no-one can possibly have recognised it.

They were regarded as bosom pals,—the only Australian players staying, for some reason, at the Hotel Richmond, where the England team were quartered. Bradman, who was a year older and currently the youngest Test centurion, discreetly reassured his companion that he need not worry about the hundred. It was sure to come. Just relax. Jackson, in his turn, addressed himself just as discreetly to umpire Hele during the lunch break, asking if he thought England would take the new ball now available. Hele replied that any captain with his head on the right way would take the new ball with his bowlers refreshed.

So, having freshened himself up, Archie Jackson strolled out onto the field of battle again to look for those three precious runs. Larwood, the mightiest fast bowler of them all, reached the end of his long run, turned, and faced the slim lad who was later to christen him, with feeling, "The Red Devil". He galloped in, accelerating. The left arm was hoisted high, the right arm screamed round in its full circle, and the new ball, glistening, flashed down on Jackson's off stump. He moved into it and with a clean sweep of the bat cracked the ball square to the cover-point fence in front of the Members' Stand before boundary fieldsman Tate could move. Archie was 101, and grinning coyly at the sensation.

The crowd went wild. Hats were tossed in the air. There was a deafening torrent of cheering as they saw their dream come true. The boy had done it! And, launching a festival of thanksgiving, Jackson, when his admirers had finally given up their throaty applause, began to slice the bowling. Duckworth once appealed for leg-before, whooping loudly, but the cry was turned down, and England's wicketkeeper heard the wrath of the crowd, yet again.

The timidity that accompanied Jackson through the morning was now gone, and he applied all his strokes one after the other with nonchalance. He lofted the ball precisely into open spaces, and cut with a cheeky wristiness that was pure Macartney. He contrived the swiftest of stolen singles. He glanced the faster balls and drove effortlessly right through the off-side arc so that the tiring bowlers—the three who had done almost all the work, and done it so tidily—must have feared the worst. Larwood padded in for over after over, now below top pace. White rolled away expressionlessly as if patrolling his Stogumber farm in Somerset. Tate, whose humour was indestructible, banged the ball into the unresponsive pitch off his short run-up, and eventually had Bradman caught for 40. They had added 82 in as many minutes, and Mailey commented that it was Bradman's bad luck to have batted with a partner, Jackson, whose brilliancy would have overshadowed any man.

With Ted a'Beckett at the crease, Archie changed his bat and took one or two deep breaths. There were signs of recklessness about him now. When he was 128 he should have been run out, except that Geary's throw was not gathered by Duckworth.

Cracking 51 runs in 49 minutes, he reached his 150 with a model late cut for three off Hammond. Then, on 164, he was leg-before trying to turn White to leg. The epic, admired as much by his opponents as by his own people, was over.

M.A.Noble awarded Jackson the palm for the "greatest knock of the series" (Hammond's notwithstanding). The only regret the crowd had was that he had not continued to prosper, particularly as he had just scored 51 in even time in a stand of 60 with a'Beckett, several times chopping over-pitched balls, with the full face of the bat, with the speed of light past second slip. P.G.H. Fender had only ever seen Macartney do this. (Fender's brief 16mm film of this Test match is frustrating because he had no "long lens". Archie Jackson's cover drive to reach his hundred therefore remains a distant blur on celluloid.)

It was over, he was exhausted, he was exhilarated. And tributes to his gallant, near-perfect innings of 164 (318 minutes; 15 fours) sprang up from all directions. The SACA presented him with a set of cut glass; some local enthusiasts gave him an inscribed travelling clock, others a rug; at home in Balmain the Mayor called a public meeting to honour him; the Methodist community of Sydney was invited to a gathering at Sydney Town Hall to "tell him what a credit he is to his country"; a bob-in (i.e. shillings) fund was started in factories and offices.

Archie Jackson thought it was all delightful, but he dreaded having to make the speeches expected of him; the prospect of having to rescue Australia's sinking innings was a simple task compared to climbing on a platform to face the listening multitude.

It began that evening, when he received a presentation on the stage of Adelaide's Garden Theatre. During the day's play he had been escorted to the Vice-Regal box to meet and talk with the distinguished State Governor, Sir Alexander Hore-Ruthven.

There was no looking back now. He was an established—not just a promising—national hero, a name in world headlines. And his 200 runs in this Test match were to remain the highest ever by an Australian batsman on debut until overtaken by Kepler Wessels (208) at the Gabba against England in 1982-83. (Oddly enough, one was born in Scotland and the other in South Africa.)

Australia finished with 369, to gain an unexpected lead of 35. When, on the fourth day, Hobbs and Sutcliffe were out for 21, England's chances rested upon the inexhaustible Hammond and his one reliable defensive partner, Douglas Jardine. They added a record 262, the value of which was revealed when the last eight wickets tumbled for 100 runs.

Jackson did not take the field after tea, 12th man Tommy Andrews substituting. But while he had been patrolling mid-off he had been called upon to stop some smoking-hot drives from Hammond, who was being attacked almost exclusively (and rather puzzlingly) down the off side.

The fifth day was another of sizzling heat: 100 degrees Fahrenheit in the shade for much of it. Again Jackson did not field.

Jardine, having negotiated Grimmett's persistent leg-side attack, lost his wicket to Oxenham when two short of a century. Hammond, through sheer tiredness, fell for 177, and it was left to Tate to lift the tail with 47 priceless runs off 50 balls.

Australia needed 349 on a pitch that was still innocent. By the fifth evening they had made 24 of them without loss, Woodfull having shielded Jackson from Larwood for most of the session.

On the sixth morning, Jackson began edgily, twice snicking White wide of Hammond's right hand. By the time Geary was brought up to strengthen the slips it was too late. The Australian openers progressed well for an hour. Jackson, who had been encouraged by the shrewd old campaigner M.A. Noble to "come out and go after" slow leftie White, was doing so with fair success—the only Australian for whom this could be claimed. One blow landed the ball on the full on the leg-side pickets, and another sent it swirling over the close field for two. Twice Chapman at silly point intercepted seemingly certain boundary strokes.

Then Woodfull walked down the pitch and had a few words with his young partner, who became subdued. He played two maiden overs from White and then, with his score 36, he was caught behind off Geary. His batting before the issuing of the caution might well have won the match for Australia. As it was, Noble's groan and heated comment were heard all over the Adelaide Press-box. (Umpire George Hele later wrote that Woodfull, far from being critical, was actually saying "Keep it up, Jacko!")

Woodfull was out soon afterwards, and Hendry fell after lunch. Ryder and Kippax raised Australia's hopes from that point, adding 137 for the fourth wicket against a tiring attack half of which always seemed to be the artful Jack White. Had he broken down there is little doubt that Australia would have cruised to their target.

They came so close. At 308 for 6 (41 needed) they were winning the battle. Then Percy Chapman dived to catch Oxenham, and nerves were stretched. When Bradman was run out for 58, 29 were still required with two wickets remaining. It was a thriller.

Chapman's field setting came in for criticism. He left the forward short-leg position, through which singles were leaking, open until after lunch, to the fury of the tacticians watching those gripping last minutes.

The match was at boiling point with 23 needed, two wickets left, when lunch was reluctantly taken. Tate bowled fierily after the break, but it was his catch, taken at the second attempt, from Grimmett's bat that cheered the English camp. By then only 13 were needed.

A fateful 13. For the last wicket fell also at that score. Forty-six year-old Don Blackie, already envisaging his popularity should he hit a pair of sixes to save the day, belted White sky-high to leg and Larwood ran like a greyhound to get under it and hugged the ball as if his future prosperity depended on it.

So England gained a 12-run victory which was all the more sublime for having taken six and a half days of cricket to achieve. Credit was reflected on both sides in an era when Anglo-Australian cricket was at a peak.

Denzil Batchelor, recalling this match in 1950, added another dimension: "You would have been little understood if you had predicted at Adelaide, 21 years ago, that last year there would be schoolboys writing to ask Bradman for his autograph, with an urgent postscript 'and please sign Sir Don'—schoolboys to whom the very name of the late Archie Jackson meant nothing at all."

A very young New South Wales side (which included a promising country lad, Stan McCabe) was selected to play MCC a week later, starting the day after the St Valentine's Day Massacre in faraway Chicago; but the first day was washed out and on the second, when play was agreed at 2.45 pm, only two English players were at the ground. Some had been inspecting the rising framework of the Sydney Harbour Bridge, some had gone to the races, others had been visiting friends, for they had all been told quite positively that there could be no chance of play before 4 o'clock.

The team were hastily gathered up and, with spinner "Tich" Freeman actually keeping wicket for the first few overs while Ames changed, MCC proceeded to sweep the State side away on a moist wicket for 128, of which Jackson, who was given a loud reception as he walked to the crease, made only 5. Kippax, for the second season running, attained the rare aggregate in Australian first-class cricket of a thousand runs.

Rain washed out the fourth day, and so, with no chance to atone for his inconsiderable failure, Jackson, after a modest performance against his old favourites South Australia, went to Melbourne for the final Test of the 1928-29 series.

It was the turn of the tide for Australia, who introduced three young players—Tim Wall, Percy Hornibrook and Alan Fairfax. England lacked their captain, Percy Chapman, who had influenza, and Herbert Sutcliffe, who had a shoulder strain. Their places were taken by Ernest Tyldesley and Maurice Leyland, the latter scoring 137 in his first Ashes Test innings, in this eight-day match, the longest ever between England and Australia.

White won the toss, but England were laborious on the first day, the highlight of which was Jack Hobbs's twelfth and final century against Australia. They batted all through the second day as well, Leyland making his hundred and several of the Australians running (or slipping) into criticism for being poorly "spiked". Jackson was one who went sprawling as he attempted to scoop up a ball on the boundary, and the offence was seen to be much more serious when he finally had the chance to bat.

England totalled 519, and Woodfull and Jackson opened very cautiously against Larwood and Tate. After 54 balls, only two runs had come. Then the tempo increased, and the score had mounted to 54 in an hour and a half when Jackson (30) slipped in starting out for a single to Larwood deep at point. The fast bowler's return to Geary was swift, and another pretty Jackson innings was over.

Woodfull went on to make a century, as did Bradman, and Australia (491) were not too far behind after all. But the runs were hard-won and the daily output was proving tiresome to a public that was probably getting too much Test cricket.

England made 257 the second time, which left Australia to make 286. They started half an hour from the end of the sixth day, with Oldfield and Hornibrook the "nightwatchmen" openers. They survived, through several near misses, until lunch-time on the seventh day, by which time 51 of the runs had been made. When the plucky Oldfield left at 80, Jackson joined Woodfull, and they saw the score to 129 after tea, at which point Woodfull was bowled—for the first time in 27 months of first-class cricket. Hammond worked the trick (though it was "played on" and not "clean bowled"), and began to make the ball kick sharply. One spiteful delivery hit Jackson in the chest; another hit wicketkeeper Duckworth in the neck. England had a real hope of achieving a five-nil whitewash.

For a time, with Kippax as his partner, Jackson postponed that hope with a series of lovely drives square and straight. But a marvellous delivery from Geary bowled him for 46 (leaving him eight short of a thousand for the season), and the fieldsmen became more sprightly as the bowlers pressed for victory.

At the end of the seventh day Australia needed 113 to win with six wickets standing.

When Kippax was run out going for a fourth run next morning the game was evenly balanced still: 82 to win, five men to fall. Bradman joined Ryder, and ought to have been stumped; but the most decisive incident was when Ryder received a questionable benefit from the umpire after Leyland had thrown the wicket down from mid-on.

Shortly after lunch the runs were made, without further loss. For Australia the taste of victory was so good. Self-respect had returned. Now it seemed that the advent of Jackson, Bradman, Fairfax, Oxenham, and Wall would stand Australia in good stead for years to come, and the perennial sadness at the termination of another Test series was matched by the expectation of a very special return rubber in England in a year's time.

As a footnote to the match, the most extraordinary spectacle occurred after the victory when, in the chaos of the celebration, no motor car could be found to take the four New South Wales players to catch their train to Sydney. In the emergency, they commandeered a horse-drawn cab, which presented an odd sight as it clopped along with Messrs Kippax, Fairfax, Bradman and Jackson squeezed inside the cabin and perched on the step and dicky-seat. It must have reminded the grinning Archie of the old Balmain laundry cart.

CHAPTER SIX

Frost on the Bloom

The Jacksons were deeply proud of their boy, and let it be known to the queue of reporters who called at Ferdinand Street for a domestic angle. His mother recalled childhood incidents which, in reality, had not taken place so very long ago. Sister Lil spoke of the tussles she had had with her brother: she, being the strongest and highest-spirited of the girls, used to take him on whenever he was in a romping mood.

"Always fighting," said mother. "We all knew he would make good at cricket ... There's not a quieter, more modest boy in Sydney ... We have to drag the words out of him ... he won't repeat things unless he's pressed ... Archie never boasts..." Then she whispered reflectively: "We won't say that he wasn't disappointed a little at the beginning of the season."

One interviewer who had managed to talk to him direct came away with the impression that "force of character is latent in him. There is no sign of aggression in his demeanour, a characteristic which has not a little to do with his popularity."

At Balmain Town Hall on May 11, 1929 he was presented with an inscribed silver tea service and a cheque for £200, the proceeds of the Testimonial. It was a gala evening, with stage skits which alluded almost monotonously to the hero of the hour. The Mayor made the presentation after a number of speeches during which one alderman reminded the citizens that Balmain, as well as being the birthplace of F.R. Spofforth (the "Demon" bowler of the 1870s and '80s), had also seen much of another early Australian cricket champion, W.L. (Billy) Murdoch.

M.A. Noble paid his tribute and Dr L.O.S. Poidevin indulged in a play on names by referring to another great Archie (MacLaren) and another great Jackson (Hon. F.S.), both fine English cricketers whose combined batting and captaincy achievements he hoped Balmain's Archie might one day emulate.

The Rev. Sam McKibbin, the local Methodist minister and a younger brother of Tom, the former Australian Test bowler, recounted his pride at having bowled Archie out years ago. Alan Kippax, more seriously and most interestingly, predicted that by the end of the 1930 tour of England Archie would be clearly the best batsman in the world.

When Archie Jackson stood to respond, the cheering lasted some time, which could not have soothed his tingling nerves.

But he maintained his composure, and in a neat little speech he thanked his admirers and friends for all they had done for him, and expressed the hope that he would be associated with Balmain for many years to come. The speech reduced him, but after the Mayor's wife had presented Mrs Jackson with a basket of flowers he came to his mother's rescue, responding on her behalf.

His popularity at times became a trial both to Archie and the family. Callers arrived at all hours, and although he was sometimes driven to asking Mum to tell them he was out, the blue De Soto sedan of which he was now the unashamedly proud owner stood in the street as an advertisement that the star was at home.

He often brought his pals in for a feed, and to some he became very attached. Arthur Allsopp, a hard-hitting batsman whose promise was never quite fulfilled, was a special friend. He was staying with the Jacksons one weekend when a cricket banquet was being held in the city, and because Allsopp had no formal clothes, Archie, who by now had the necessary dress for such occasions, refused to go either. The problem was overcome by adapting Mr Jackson's navy pinstripe suit, blackening Allsopp's brown shoes, and pinning on a makeshift bow-tie. (The only real vanity ever observed in Archie was a muttered dread of baldness; in clothes he preferred casual styles.)

On a less happy occasion another "friend" stayed at the house overnight, and when Archie paid a visit next day to the dentist (Australian Test batsman Johnny Taylor) he discovered that his trouser pockets had been cleared out. Such money as came his way he did not squander.

He knew the value of a shilling after the deprivations of past years. And as the Great Depression later bit into the economy and his father's earnings diminished he pledged himself never to allow his mother to go to work.

He played only five first-class matches and had only five innings (360 runs at 72) for Balmain the following season, 1929-30, when ill-health began to stalk him. He was hugely successful in all bar one of the major fixtures, and was never other than an automatic choice for the England tour.

He began with an 80 at Brisbane, and two centuries of varying significance at Sydney. The first was an attractive 108 not out against A.H.H. Gilligan's MCC team on their way to New Zealand. Though he made the runs off a depleted attack he treated the veteran Frank Woolley's slow left-arm bowling with no great respect, and stood up well to the fast deliveries of Maurice Allom, who was to take four wickets in five balls a few weeks later in a Test match at Christchurch. Jackson's hundred came in a mere two and a quarter hours when he pulled a no-ball from Woolley for four. Against loose bowling he scored thereafter at a run a minute till the declaration.

It was a high-scoring match: Bradman, Kippax and Allsopp (in his first first-class innings) all made centuries and the budding champion McCabe hit 90; and for MCC Maurice Turnbull made 100 and Woolley 219. So bizarre was the final innings of this drawn match that Jackson was called upon to bowl four overs, which realised 28 runs.

But it was in the next match, billed as a Test Trial, that he played the classic innings of the season—some said of his lifetime. The sides—Ryder's XI and Woodfull's XI—contained, for the first time ever, players from all six States of the Commonwealth. Jackson was among those players who must have felt that they were not exactly on trial; at least, he opened the match with remarkable confidence, driving everything up to him with a freedom that amounted almost to indifference.

The day was warm, and five thousand people were present when Tim Wall stormed in from the Paddington end to start proceedings. Boundaries were soon coming with regularity from Jackson, but Ponsford was watchful. The only hitch came when Fairfax hit Jackson on the left knee, dashing to his aid as he lurched around in agony. Soon Archie was hitting Blackie through long-off then lofting his off-breaks to the long-on boundary. In due course a slashing hit off the same bowler brought up the hundred and at lunch, after 100 minutes' play, the total was 122: Jackson 81, Ponsford 41 (including one boundary shot that uprooted a picket from the fence).

In the afternoon Jackson again powerfully drove the cunning Blackie, and it was remarked that seldom had he driven with such gusto. He reached 99, and stroked Blackie straight, but the bowler intercepted. Two balls later he thrust him through point for another boundary, his fifteenth, and another glorious century was his.

Nor did he wilt there. The Tasmanian, Arthur Burrows, was called into the attack, and Jackson took 15 off his first over, one straight-drive whistling through the bowler's desperate fingers. Old Don Blackie continued to suffer as he had never suffered before. Jackson cracked his offspin mercilessly, going down on one knee and swinging him to the leg fence.

Ponsford began to pepper the field too, and the score moved from 150 to 200 in twenty minutes. The crowd had built up to ten thousand by then, and pleased they were to see Jackson hoist the steady Hornibrook for a straight six. A single off Wall, who was still occasionally getting the ball to kick head-high, made him 150.

His mate Fairfax came on at the Randwick end, and he grinned teasingly as he cut him twice for fours to reach 170, his highest score in first-class cricket. Off the seventh ball he square-drove another flashing four. Where would it end? No bowler could logically hope to defeat him. Ponsford, the record-breaker, was batting exceptionally well, but he was sidelined by Jackson's magnificence.

Eventually he swung carelessly at Hornibrook and missed, then skyed the next to cover, where Kippax, his mentor, took the catch. The stand of 278 had lasted 187 minutes, and Jackson's 182 included 27 fours and a six. Again a long, hyperactive innings had taken much out of him.

It was possibly during this contest that a poignant incident occurred. One of Jackson's team-mates was Alec Marks. Over sixty years later, his son Neil, a very talented New South Wales batsman himself, included this anecdote in his book *Tales from the Locker Room*: Archie Jackson had forgotten to pack a towel, so he borrowed one from Alec Marks. When Alec returned home his mother gave him an earful for not bringing the towel back: it was top quality, and they were in the midst of the Great Depression. Next day, Alec asked Archie for the towel, but instead of returning it, he gave him a brand new one, with no explanation. Unhappily, Alec's mother was not satisfied, perceiving the replacement as inferior in quality. "I can't understand Archie's behaviour. He always seemed like such a nice boy."

A few years later, when Archie was fighting for his life in a Brisbane hospital, Alec Marks was among his many visitors. As he was about to leave, Marks at last heard the explanation: "Acka, do you remember the towel you gave me that day?" said Jackson. "It was your Mum's best guest towel and I didn't return it." Marks assured him that it didn't matter, but the explanation came nonetheless: he knew then that he had tuberculosis; so he made a point of never lending or borrowing clothing or gear. "But that particular day, when you threw me your towel, I dried myself without thinking. I didn't realise what I'd done until I returned home. That's why I bought you a new one. The man behind the counter said it was the best towel in the shop. I hope your Mum liked it." "Archie," said Alec, choking up, "Mum said it was the best towel she ever owned." Neil Marks continued: "When he came home my father walked to his mother's linen-closet and took out the towel Archie had bought. Then he sat down on his bed, put his head into it, and cried."

After Archie's memorable 182 in that Test Trial at Sydney, the score continued to mount, reaching 663. Woodfull's team were then shot out by spinners Oxenham and Grimmett for 309 and followed on; but the unstoppable Bradman added a double-century to his first-innings century, and Kippax stroked 170 in celebration at having overthrown recent illness. Ryder's side went in needing 188.

This time Jackson was kept back to No.7 and the "youngsters" batted ahead of him. Trouble lay ahead: the cagey spinners Hornibrook and Blackie wove their spell on a rain-damaged pitch. Stan McCabe was easily top-scorer with 46; Jackson was caught behind for 15; and it was left to Ryder and Grimmett to scrape the winning runs with nine down.

It may well have been during this match that Archie Jackson's grey-blue eyes fell upon a crippled boy on crutches who sat watching other lads playing cricket on the broad expanse of Moore Park. The boy explained that on account of his disability he was not allowed to play. "Will you be here tomorrow?" Archie asked him, and the next morning he brought an autographed bat along for him and played with him till it was time to prepare for the big match. Understandably the gesture was never forgotten.

Just before Christmas, New South Wales had a reversal at Adelaide. South Australia amassed 508 and Clarrie Grimmett did the rest; but the newcomers, Stan McCabe and Arthur Allsopp, both made runs in both innings, and a further bright spot was the opening partnership between Bradman and Jackson in the second innings. Facing arrears of 194, they placed 172 on the board before Bradman was leg-before to Grimmett. He had taken an unsavoury knock in the stomach from Wall early in the innings, but this did not upset his plan of stepping out to Grimmett while most batsmen played back cautiously.

Jackson, neat and unruffled as ever, once swung a Grimmett full-toss into the stand for six, and showed during his 82 that he was in every sense a master batsman. Bradman, for all his efficiency, was recognised as having a "resource that made up for what he lacked in grace".

His alleged lack of grace was almost beside the point early in the New Year as he compiled a new world-record score of 452 not out at Sydney against Queensland. To anyone who might have overlooked the fact, D.G. Bradman was positively and irrevocably a world name—a maker rather than a gatherer of runs, always "a better batsman than the other fellow is a bowler", never satisfied with a century or even a double-century so long as his team occupied the crease. Some Englishmen may have been sceptical of the angle of his bat, but it usually came down straight, usually met the ball centrally, and usually was raised aloft every hour or so to acknowledge the applause for another 50 runs.

The national selectors had no grounds for hesitation over his name or several others when they drew up their list for England. It was simply a matter of filling the last four or five places.

Archie Jackson missed the Victoria match at Melbourne as well as Bradman's fortissimo 452 in the Queensland match, and also the home fixture against South Australia. The vicious seed of tuberculosis was in him, though it was not yet fully understood. He had been forced into hospital in Adelaide after the Christmas match there, and the authorities began to feel concern for him. The problem was listed as "poorness of blood and an outbreak of boils".

He returned for the Victoria match at Sydney, but made only 5 in a rain-ruined interlude that forced the selectors to postpone their final choice for England.

Soon, however, the names were announced amid the customary mixture of jubilation and heartbreak: W.M.

Woodfull (captain), V.Y. Richardson (vice-captain), A.F. Kippax, D.G. Bradman, A.A. Jackson, S.J. McCabe, A.G. Fairfax, W.A. Oldfield, W.H. Ponsford, E.L. a'Beckett, C.V. Grimmett, T.W. Wall, C.W. Walker, P.M. Hornibrook, and A. Hurwood.

Balmain responded with another "bob-in" appeal (donations of a shilling), which raised for their hero the very considerable sum of £212, a hundred of which was handed to Mrs Jackson by her grateful son as contribution towards a new house in Drummoyne. Dad, true to form, had put in his shilling without comment when a collector approached him without knowing who he was. And at a Balmain "smoko" at the Town Hall, Archie was presented with a cabin wardrobe.

The Board of Control, as one of its main preparatory tasks, arranged for Jackson to have his tonsils removed. Ponsford had suffered from tonsillitis on the previous tour in 1926, and the Board was anxious to prevent a similar occurrence. But the Jackson family would always regard the operation as having been needless. Archie had never been troubled by his tonsils. Indeed his only remembered sicknesses had been childhood ailments, such as mumps, measles, chickenpox.

Dr Reg Bettington, who played cricket for New South Wales and Middlesex and was a triple Blue at Oxford, was in practice as an ear, nose and throat specialist in Manly, and it was he who performed the surgery. It affected Jackson adversely, as the family recall. He lost a stone in weight, and became even more poorly after catching a chill in Tasmania, where the touring team played two matches.

But it was a leisured age, and after crossing Australia by

means of a very long and tedious train journey, and playing against Western Australia, the team travelled by ship—not aircraft—to Britain. This allowed the cricketers to get to know each other and helped assuage the wear and tear of the past season.

It also gave Archie the opportunity to win the peg quoits competition, much to his own amusement. It was fun and games the whole way, with an off-beat episode in Ceylon when the team, wearing unfamiliar solar topees (pith helmets), played a Colombo side. Rain, that seemed to follow them across the world, curtailed the match.

They disembarked at Naples and crammed in a lot of European sightseeing (including some uninhibited snowball fights—film survives) before confronting the sublime vision of Dover's white cliffs. Australians of that era used to refer to this as "coming Home".

CHAPTER SEVEN

England, 1930

"If the Australian team has no Macartney it will at least have Archie Jackson," promised the *Sydney Mail*, whose observer went on to say that Bradman and Jackson, to judge from their fresh, smooth faces, might both have been undergraduates instead of tempered heroes of a score of classic innings against some of the best bowling in the world. (Not so long ago, the 15-year-old Archie, and his mate Bill Hunt, had travelled in a train to Chatswood for a grade match and failed to identify the great Charlie Macartney sitting opposite them in the carriage.)

The *Sydney Mail* had already lodged a quite astounding claim on Jackson's behalf: "On Australian wickets, and judged solely on stroke technique, Archie Jackson may be justifiably regarded as the greatest of present-day batsmen—greater even than Walter Hammond.... He was not forced, as was Hammond repeatedly, to look for runs in one direction."

Jackson's reputation travelled well ahead of him, and all eyes were on him at the preliminary net practices at Lord's. Indeed, all eyes had been on him when *Orford* landed the players at Dover, as were those of a woman correspondent who quoted him as being against cricketers' wives touring with them. "When we're not playing," he told her, "I just want to go round London by myself. I love London. I saw the rain the day we arrived and the sun yesterday and today, and I like them both."

She had a scoop, for the *Daily Chronicle* man had ruefully to report that "a younger and handsomer lot have never before come in quest of the Ashes—nor one more silent.... Silence with them, however, is both legal and compulsory. Each man carries a formidable legal document."

Lord Harris, who had captained England against Australia before any of this team had been born, welcomed them as they disembarked, eleven of the fifteen stepping onto English soil for the first time (assuming the infant Scot Archie Jackson had never been taken south of the border). They faced a battery of cameras and questions, and most of the crowd seemed astounded at their overall youthfulness.

One observer painted a graphic picture of the young Aussies: "These bronzed, keen-eyed, spare athletes are for the greater part a team of boys. If you put players like McCabe, Jackson, Bradman and Walker in school caps they would be almost like the enthusiastic boys who will hunt them all summer in search of forbidden autographs."

Autographs were indeed banned, at least at Lord's, and soon the Australians were being told by manager W.L. Kelly that they should cease to give autographs altogether, a rather mean instruction that was sometimes ignored. Kelly himself apparently became extremely friendly with the woman who was manager at the team's London hotel headquarters, and inspired little respect from some of his players as the tour progressed. However, he did at least take some movie footage during the tour, now tucked away somewhere on the Internet under Charles Henshall donations.

A huge crowd had been building up outside Victoria Station for over an hour to greet the touring cricketers as the boat-train arrived. As Vic Richardson recalled in his autobiography, (*The Vic Richardson Story*, 1967) when Australia's Prime Minister James Scullin arrived in London later that summer it was, in contrast, days before his presence became public knowledge.

They stayed at London's Midland Grand Hotel, St Pancras, and the first official engagement was the High Commissioner's welcome at Australia House. When Sir Granville Ryrie had finished with them they went on to the Savoy Hotel for a reception by the British Sportsman's Club, with the Duke of Gloucester in attendance. King George V's message of greeting was read out, Lord Harris toasted them, Woodfull responded, then they continued on to Lord's for a light work-out in the fresh spring air.

The big occasions mounted up: the laying of a wreath at St Clement Dane's Church on Anzac Day (with Jackson, Bradman and Fairfax going on to the National Liberal Club for dinner and billiards); a formal Gala Performance in their honour at the Coliseum (with Archie Jackson looking even younger in a dinner jacket than in flannels); and—the greatest of thrills for him—seats just behind the King's box at Wembley for the FA Cup final between Huddersfield Town and Arsenal, when the German airship, the Graf Zeppelin, put in an eerie appearance over the packed stadium.

The net practices continued as reminders of the purpose of their tour, and the forecasts and analyses proliferated. The *Evening News* spy saw Bradman, in his bright blue New South Wales cap, make a "few preliminary flourishes", then Jackson unwittingly lured the entire audience to himself. All the MCC ground-staff boys gathered, and 'Plum' Warner escorted his young son across to see the youthful wonder from Australia.

Jackson gave them all the strokes: the swish off the toes, the late cut, and the square drive which everyone seemed to have heard about. Then Grimmett spun a couple of googlies through him and grinned. Jackson nodded his appreciation.

"He looks," the *News* correspondent noted neatly, "like any English public school boy, is quiet, and a little shy. There is something of the Hobbs about Jackson, the stylist."

Geoffrey Tebbutt, who covered the tour for Australian Press Association, put it this way: "The English, who worship style in horses, dogs, evening clothes, and batting, got ready to acclaim young Jackson."

Somerset's M.D. "Dar" Lyon, another keen observer, wrote in *The Daily Sketch*: "Jackson looked about the best bat to me. He is a little on the short side, but obviously strong and supple." Supple he always was; but his strength was fast becoming an illusion.

Things went wrong from the start. Bouts of illness were so persistent that he even missed some enticing social functions.

And he was generally uneasy on the damp, greenish pitches. It has become a familiar problem: the look and feel of English wickets in April and May can so easily instil an unreasoning apprehension into the mind of a young visiting batsman who is accustomed to reliable batting surfaces.

No such phobia troubled Don Bradman, who had an utterly sensational tour, having built for himself the advantage of a roaring start (236, 185, 78) free of the misfortune of being caught miraculously at the start of an innings.

Jackson's first innings, against Worcestershire, ended in such a way. He had been far from certain, especially against Fred Root's in-duckers; but, swinging hard at a poor-length ball from George Brook, he was mortified to see Cyril Walters conjure a catch at forward short leg.

He failed at Leicester, although Jack Hobbs wrote of him flatteringly. And batting No.5 against Essex in bitterly cold weather, he made some charming strokes in the second innings before being caught off his "chop shot". It was here at Leyton that some newsreel film of the Australians was shot. Through the wonders of the Internet we are now able to find clips of him in a number of sources: batting, standing, throwing snowballs, invariably smiling rather self-consciously among groups of players. Clarrie Grimmett's 1930 tour film has also recently been edited and published. But it's to be lamented that there seems to have been no recording of Archie's voice.

In glimpses, Archie Jackson was showing the English public a sample of his culture. But he was not making centuries, or even half-centuries.

There came a happy interlude when he met his cousin James

in Liverpool. Their fathers were brothers, and James's sire had returned with Sandy from Australia the first time and remained in Scotland. For years there had been no contact, but young James, who captained the renowned Liverpool Football Club, had taken it upon himself while laid up with a knee injury to enquire if this young Australian cricketer could possibly be his cousin. He was, and he was granted a day's leave to visit. James Jackson played professional soccer in order to finance his studies to enter the church, and was known to the football crowds as "The Parson".

While in Liverpool, several of the players tried unsuccessfully to telephone relatives in Sydney, but they had more luck a week later in London, Jackson and Fairfax speaking to family, friends and club-mates and hearing them quite clearly in return.

Off Lancashire's bowling, Jackson made a pleasant 40, hooking well, and drawing a further expert opinion on his style, this time from the irrepressible Cecil Parkin: "He is perhaps a little slow—a Conservative at the crease. But he may become a batting Bolshevik any time. It is my opinion that he is a better bat than Bradman."

The team returned to London for the MCC match—Archie's first appearance at Lord's. In front of a capacity house he made a duck, caught behind off tall fast bowler Maurice Allom. In the second innings he was criticised for poor running and backing up, and was even blamed for Woodfull's downfall, the skipper tumbling over after being sent back and, with his arm hurt, playing the ball into his stumps shortly afterwards. But Jackson managed his first fifty of the tour, reached with a sweetly on-driven six off leg-spinner G.T.S. Stevens, and went on to a carefully-made 64 before Patsy Hendren picked him up brilliantly at slip.

Still there was dissatisfaction and disappointment. Charlie Macartney, who was covering the tour for the *Mirror* and now knew the young man quite well, was concerned at the absence of freedom in his strokeplay. And though there had been universal pleasure after lunch when he "almost revealed his old self" Archie still seemed cramped much of the time.

It was looking better for him in the near-freezing conditions at Chesterfield, where he and Ponsford opened with 127. He was all at sea against Tommy Mitchell's leg-spin, but weathered the spell and actually on-drove him on the full for six. Later he landed Townsend into the pavilion. But he failed against Surrey, "hanging his bat out ingloriously", and followed that with nought against Hampshire in the match in which, in pouring rain, Bradman achieved his thousand runs by the end of May.

Then came Lord's again, the Middlesex match, when Archie showed truer touch without making many runs. He actually came in for some barracking during a tedious period, which was almost certainly an unprecedented experience for him. Percy Hornibrook remembered his reaction: "Be damned—I'll show them!" And he refused to make a shot for several overs, a rare show of petulance from one so extraordinarily even-tempered.

At least, as Bradman and Jackson shared a modest stand, a worried 'Plum' Warner was moved to see them as "names destined to appear on the scoresheet for many a long year." What bliss there is in our blindness to events as yet undisclosed.

During the Cambridge University match the players were invited to Sandringham Castle to meet the King and Queen, but Archie had been unwell again and had to miss what for some was the highlight of the summer. He was never one to complain.

By now the first Test was imminent, and Arthur Mailey made a poignant plea in the *Daily Herald* for his protégé's selection, urging it if for no other reason than that his great ability was now undoubted: "Jackson is a match-winner, and I am sure he will yet thrill and surprise the English cricket public by his artistry and technique."

But with most of the batsmen in fair form there was no real case for including a man so much out of touch that he was seen defensively halfway back on his right leg before the bowler's arm came over.

The Australians conditioned themselves for the first Test by withdrawing in secrecy to Downside School, and it was there that a reporter peeped through the hedge and saw Jackson and Wall playing a vigorous game of tennis. For Wall, who was in the team, it served as a distracting loosener. For Jackson, 12th man, it offered a chance to let off steam.

England won the Trent Bridge Test by 93 runs, but it was to be the only defeat suffered by the Australians throughout the tour. The baggage was all shifted back to London for the Surrey match, and by now two bags stood out conspicuously. They belonged to Kippax and Jackson (obviously from the sports shop) and were each adorned with four handles and painted yellow and green all over. "Seemingly big enough to accommodate a kangaroo," thought one gaping onlooker.

It was reported at this time that Jackson's illness had at first been thought serious, but he was now back in the side, making 37 not out, driving well, and looking more like the batsman of the previous Australian season.

He made 52 against Lancashire, late-cutting well and having some overdue luck. Hodgson, who struck him in the chest early in the innings, finally knocked his off stump back.

He had not done enough to find a place in the second Test, at Lord's, though he went to Blackpool beforehand to "tone up" with some members of the team and a group of the Lancashire players. Other diversions included golf at the West Kent course, and mini-cricket with a Woolworths bat and golf ball on the lawn of some new friends at Bickley.

The Lord's Test match was a classic, made even more memorable by the sight of the R101 airship as it loomed overhead—an ill-starred giant that was to crash in flames the day the Australians sailed for home.

K.S. Duleepsinhji and captain Percy Chapman made centuries for England, but 155 by Woodfull and a famous and impeccable 254 by Bradman ensured an eventual seven-wicket victory for Australia that levelled the series. Amazingly, it's believed that Archie almost played in this match when Bradman was late to arrive on the opening morning. He was actually getting changed as The Don came flying up the stairs.

Jackson now uncovered better form. In the acid test of the Yorkshire match at Bradford his 46 contained some scintillating strokes, and though he made only a third of the runs in a stand of 138 with Ponsford, hopes were rising.

Next came Nottinghamshire, and scores of 22 and 79.

But the most significant events were Fairfax's admission to hospital for an operation and Ponsford's sudden attack of gastritis. This left the vacancy which Jackson might have forced in any case. He was chosen for the third Test, at Headingley, Leeds, which pleased, among many, Neville Cardus, then writing as "Cricketer" in the Manchester *Guardian*. He had been fascinated by Archie Jackson at Old Trafford: "Somehow Jackson gave us a flavour. He is an enigma on English cricket fields, so far. You can feel intuitively that he is a cultured batsman; every now and again he lets us see a stroke that none but the elect can ever hope to perform. Checked action, born of no confidence, is at present hindering the gush of his quality. Woodfull ought to keep him in the XI until class has come forth, as sooner or later class will."

Recalling the best of Australian batsmen—Trumper, Hill, Macartney, Syd Gregory, Ransford, Joe Darling—he reminded readers and players alike that "the scoreboard was not their eternal looking-glass."

Archie Jackson's part in the third Test match was soon over. Opening with his captain, he made but one run before being caught at short leg by Larwood off Tate (film survives). Bradman replaced him and carved out his Ashes record 334; Kippax made 77; Australia amassed 566; and then a painstaking century by Hammond (together with rain and bad-light stoppages) deprived Australia of victory.

Jackson was also deprived of a second innings by England's follow-on just when those with active memories were wondering what devilish punishment he might unleash—as he had so often second time round. His only further chance to distinguish himself was when Tate lofted Grimmett to long-on and the catch was safely pouched.

Trevor Wignall of the *Daily Express* had seen Jackson at the Queen's Hotel just after breakfast on the first morning of the match, and could not help noticing his tenseness. He attributed Archie's failure more to anxiety than anything else.

Wignall saw much of him off the field, and was impressed by his gentleness, sincerity . . . and absentmindedness. Not only did he frequently mislay his batting-gloves or his shirt, but he even overlooked an official invitation to luncheon at the House of Commons—an oversight that upset him when it was pointed out. By the end of the tour Wignall was certain that Archie Jackson's nervous little cough had grown appreciably in strength.

From Leeds they visited Scotland for two matches in a misty and damp July. In the first, at Edinburgh, Jackson did not bat, but at Glasgow, in a match against a Scottish XI, he spent over two hours batting on what was actually his native turf, compiling a 52 not out that brought him a special satisfaction. The following day he wrote to Bill Hunt over in Sydney from the Palatine Hotel in Sunderland, the handwriting even and elegant as ever, the mood unquenchably cheerful:

> We are having a splendid time over here and I would like to stay on for a few months after our tour ends. Today we are scheduled to play Durham but it has rained so heavily that the match was abandoned. We have just concluded our trip to Scotland and everyone had a marvellous time. Of course I had some relatives there and had to look them up. They were living at Gourock, a small village twenty miles from Glasgow on the River Clyde, and we had a wonderful view of many

famous Lochs and beauty spots such as Dunoon, where Harry Lauder resides, Rothesay, Loch Long, and Loch Lomond.

Scotland is indeed a beautiful country, and I intend to spend a week there in September. I expect to see some of the big soccer matches, so that I am in Liverpool with my cousin James, who captains the Liverpool team. The two matches I shall see will be against Blackburn Rovers and Huddersfield Town.

Last month I paid a visit to Wimbledon and saw the world's best tennis players in action, viz Tilden, Cochet, Borotra, Crawford, Helen Wills, Miss Ryan, etc. I consider Tilden to be the best of them all. He is a great player indeed.

We have been playing quite a lot of tennis and golf lately. It is, after all, a spell from cricket, isn't it? And one needs a rest from the mental side of the game. I am doing better now with the bat than when we first arrived in England, and have now scored 650 runs at an average of 35.00 so that if I can maintain my form or exceed it I should total between 1300 and 1400 runs.

He then congratulated Bill on doing well for Balmain, expressing the hope that he would get in the New South Wales team in the new season, and extended best wishes to him and his fiancée Ann.

There was no undercurrent of dissatisfaction or frustration in this private letter, which could easily have served as a ready medium for someone needing to pour out the bitterness, the excuses, the exasperation.

Could it have been that he was not really all that concerned? The laboured innings seem to discount that conjecture. There seems but one conclusion: he kept it all to himself. He would not have been the first nor the last touring cricketer to sob a little in the solitude of a hotel room.

"What does it matter, as long as we win?" Archie remarked to Bradman after learning of his exclusion from the fourth Test, at Old Trafford. But he missed very little. Rain and poor light cut hours from the match, and neither side batted twice.

It was a relief to move on to the West Country, the more so when Jackson and Bradman joined forces to pulverise the Somerset bowling. They added 231 runs, and at last—at long last—Archie Jackson reached a hundred. The Taunton sun, it was said, had thawed him out.

He owed a lot to Arthur Wellard for dropping him early, but no-one could dispute that his luck was overdue. The first half of his innings was as tame and laboured as the second half was spirited. He was in for four hours and finished with 118, with fifteen fours, several off his 1928-29 adversary Jack White. It was a very popular success.

Perhaps he was lifted by a "good luck" cable from home, inspired by Dr Evatt, who requested at the annual meeting of the Balmain club that a vote of confidence be rendered. In his speech he had offered the theory that the continual changing from opener to middle-order batsman might have upset Jackson's approach.

He made a few runs against Glamorgan on the brand new pitch at St Helens, and at Northampton, when the Australians followed on, he compiled a lovely 52, after having twisted an ankle in trying to save a boundary.

By now he had worked his way back into the Test side for the final encounter, at The Oval. Though it was impossible to foresee, it was to be his last Test match against England.

He took Vic Richardson's place (one report stated that it was at Richardson's own suggestion), as he had done at Adelaide for his first Test match. But the more surprising changes were in the England side, where 42-year-old "Dodge" Whysall came in as an extra batsman, Gloucestershire's penetrative off-spinner Goddard was omitted, and there was a change of captaincy: Percy Chapman, whose effervescent leadership had taken England to six successive victories over Australia from 1926 to 1930, was now viewed by the selectors as too volatile and flamboyant for what was likely to be a grim decider (his tough line at Brisbane in 1928 apparently forgotten).

Bob Wyatt took over, and received at least one threat on his life for his—or the selectors'—temerity. It was Wyatt's partnership with the cool, determined Herbert Sutcliffe (161) that salvaged England's innings. The captain came in at 197 for 5 and weathered a nerve-tingling period, the stand of 170 enabling England to go on past 400 before Grimmett wrapped up the innings.

Jackson had distinguished himself so far with good ground fielding and throwing, once hurtling head-first into the crowd after chasing a boundary hit. There were gasps all round, but no serious injury, and the spectators concerned were left "proudly displaying the bruises they earned in the great match".

Australia replied forcefully, reaching 0/159 by tea on the second day, after which Ponsford's unlucky number—110 (made in only 135 minutes) yet again proved to be his downfall. In the gloom and after having been taken ill at the adjournment, he was bowled by the tall leg-spinner Ian Peebles, another Scottish-born cricketer. Now Bradman came to the crease, having made 742 runs already in six Test innings this summer.

A shower drove the players in immediately, but they soon returned—this time for the batsmen to appeal against the dullness. They were off for half an hour. Soon after resumption Peebles had Woodfull caught behind. That made it 190 for 2 —evenly poised as Kippax joined Bradman.

England pressed, but could make no further headway on a pitch that was offering little to the bowlers. At the end of the third day Australia were 215 for 2, still 190 behind.

Runs came steadily on the Tuesday, even when Larwood and Tate used the new ball. Then Peebles struck again, this time having Kippax nicely caught by Wyatt at short leg for 28: 263 for 3.

Archie Jackson negotiated the steps and strode out across the grass, arguing with his nerves the whole way. He and Bradman, a young pair who in tandem had made stacks of runs over the past two years, were facing a critical situation. The runs had to be made in this first innings as the pitch was fully expected to favour spin in the later stages.

Peebles bowled, and Jackson drove him wide of mid-off and scampered off for his first run: Hobbs swooped across from cover, picked up the ball and in one movement underarmed it at the bowler's stumps with Jackson still yards from home. Peebles had no chance of getting back to gather it, so swift had been the interception, and the ball bounced past its target. Lucky Jackson even had time to run an overthrow as he ruminated on the early demise he'd just escaped.

Peebles was bowling beautifully. A perfect-length googly beat Jackson, and the leg stump, and keeper Duckworth too, and went for four byes. Time and again Jackson took the spin bowler on the pad. It was a fascinating and rare duel between Scots.

Several critics considered that Jackson used his pads in defence rather too often. But he swung the bat to good purpose just before lunch, on-driving firmly for four and bisecting the outfielders with a juicy pull stroke. He and Bradman seemed to be winning the initiative as the bails were lifted for lunch.

Resumption was delayed after a downpour, and while the pitch soaked up the rain the two not-out batsmen had a genial conversation with the Prince of Wales (future short-term King Edward VIII), whose visit to the ground had been timed badly for cricket-watching but ideally for the young Australians.

It was past three before play started, and Wyatt immediately called up Larwood and Tate. On the damp but firm pitch they created few problems for the moment. Jackson showed discretion in leaving certain balls alone, but one which he did hit damaged his bat, and one of the Australians caused amusement by bringing him four replacements. He made his selection and continued to pick up singles through the infield.

Peebles eventually took over from Larwood, and Hammond from Tate: England now found the probing combination. Hammond, who always came fast off the pitch, bowled just the right length and found the spite that had eluded the other bowlers. He made one delivery kick head-high to Jackson. Backs straightened. He smashed him on the glove with the next, and then on the wrist, knocking the bat from his hand. By the time the batsman had recovered, the sky was overcast, and soon after the 400 had been raised the umpires acceded to a light appeal at 3.52pm.

Rain fell, then the sun came out, and as the evening wore on the captains made two pitch inspections, Wyatt wanting to play, Woodfull not in agreement. It seemed there would be no further cricket when, to general amazement, a re-start was ordained for twenty-five past six—which offered one over, two at best.

Bradman and Jackson unenthusiastically made their way to the middle midst cat-calls, and survived thirteen balls from Hammond and Peebles. With a measure of relief they took Australia to the shelter of 403 for 3, Bradman 130 and Jackson 43, the stand so far worth an estimable 140.

There was no rain during the night, but a heavy dew was noticeable next morning when the youngsters resumed, against Hammond and England's "baby", the 22-year-old Peebles. Seven singles came from the first eight overs, and a sprinkling of rain ceased before the fleeing players had reached the pavilion.

Jackson was poised on 49 for a long time and seemed indifferent about it before hooking left-arm spinner Leyland and running four. But Bradman cruised past his 150, and the serenity of the situation was disturbed only by a raucous appeal by George Duckworth which seemed to startle everyone, so unrealistic was any thought that a wicket might fall.

But something strange happened at noon: the Oval pitch livened up almost supernaturally, and Hammond suddenly was able to make the ball cut and kick. Larwood came into the attack (Jackson sending Bradman scrambling desperately back into his crease from the first ball) and he too created alarming bounce off a good length. He produced an extra yard of speed in his delight at the feel of a pitch that, for once, wasn't docile from over-preparation.

A cynic wrote that "neither batsman was anxious to run a sharp single in order to secure the privilege of playing him", but whenever Jackson faced up, though he took frequent shuddering blows to the body, it was noticeable that he moved into line and never shirked.

Aubrey Faulkner, the masterly South African all-rounder, who was to gas himself three weeks later, applauded the courage of both batsmen as the wicket turned hostile. Jackson, he noted, was hit on the elbow, the jaw, the hip and several times on the thighs; and he learned later that the bruises formed a black-and-blue pattern. If anything, he thought that Jackson allowed himself to be hit too often for a batsman of his class.

It was a fateful session, for Don Bradman's undisguised discomfort against Larwood, his desperate evasion of the flyers (especially after a sickening blow under the heart when he had made 175), and his reduced effectiveness combined to ignite hope in the minds of those Englishmen—not least Douglas Jardine—who had wondered in vain how on earth this Australian run machine could ever be contained.

It is recorded that Archie Jackson told friends that George Duckworth was the first to draw attention to Bradman's hesitancy, and the scheming of the Bodyline campaign apparently began at that point. Percy Fender, the Surrey and England allrounder, watched with fascination and later informed his friend and colleague Douglas Jardine. The future Ashes captain saw some footage for himself in the newsreel cinema shortly afterwards and conceived the idea of "Bodyline". Two years later, with a grotesque leg-side field placement, he unleashed Larwood, Voce and Bowes upon an unsuspecting Australian batting line-up to shape the most sensational Test series in history.

Bradman's concern extended beyond his own person this day at The Oval, for he frequently hurried to comfort his battered partner and to smack the shallow divot back into the pitch. Together they held on, and as suddenly as it had grown murderous the pitch became quiet once more, no matter how beefily the fast bowlers plunged the ball into it.

Still there were glimpses of the best of Archie Jackson, and still he had periodic anxieties, as when he cocked a ball between the wicketkeeper and Larwood at short leg, each leaving it to the other. Finally, looking for his ninth boundary, but hampered by the bruised wrist, he swung imperfectly at a leg-break from Wyatt and was caught by Sutcliffe at extra cover.

The fourth-wicket partnership of 243 surpassed the record established in 1896 by Syd Gregory and Harry Trott, and Jackson's brave and painfully disciplined 73 had helped the score to 506. His innings—and the stand—had lasted four and a half hours, and if ever an effort was worth more than face value this was it.

In a latterday book on the 1930 series, Christopher Hilton laid out the ball-by-ball scoring, as shown in *The Cricketer*, and it makes remarkable reading. Of the 311 balls faced by Archie Jackson, 266 were what moderns call "dot balls" (not scored from). His patience was bordering on the phenomenal. Against

Larwood, Tate, Peebles, Hammond, Leyland and Wyatt, he blocked persistently or let the ball go, with many a maiden over.

Bradman went on to 232 (and a series aggregate of 974 runs—still a world record just on 90 years later—at 139.14) before debatably being given out caught behind off Larwood. The two young New South Welshmen had served their country wonderfully well.

McCabe added a daring 54, and Australia amassed 695—a lead of 290. There was one poignant moment that evening when the 47-year-old Jack Hobbs came out to play his final innings in Test cricket and played on to a ball from Alan Fairfax for 9. England's sorrow was complete, after a blank fifth day, when Hornibrook (7/92) bowled them out on the worn pitch.

So Australia recaptured the Ashes on Bill Woodfull's 33rd birthday, and youth had triumphed quite brilliantly over experience. It was Australia's first Test victory at The Oval since the original "Ashes match" back in 1882, and the cheers that greeted the appearance of Woodfull and his men on the pavilion balcony at the end rivalled those in the earlier historic contest. And lest Archie's body blows be forgotten, a newspaper cartoon depicted him, bearded in old age, recalling his innings for the benefit of a small boy: "I got 73 runs and 540 knocks!"

He played five more matches in that summer of 1930, but was still anything but fluent. In the thriller with Gloucestershire which followed the final Test, the Australians needed only 118 to win. It seemed a foregone conclusion when Jackson and McCabe made half of them for the first wicket, but the remaining wickets collapsed for a further 58 against Charlie

Parker and Tom Goddard, and the result was that hilarious rarity: a tie.

Archie Jackson had further pleasant associations with Bristol to recall, for on the Sunday he made his first flight in an aeroplane, at the local Aero Club, and topped it off by presenting a floral horseshoe to Winifred Brown, who had recently won the King's Cup.

The match at Canterbury was blessed by hot weather and a wonderful demonstration of leg-spin bowling by Kent's "Tich" Freeman. At one stage in the second innings the Australians were defending for their lives on a wearing pitch, and the parents of the boys and girls who had accompanied Bradman and Jackson excitedly to the wicket were soon barracking the batsmen. But the match was saved comfortably by a Bradman double-century and 50 not out by Archie Jackson, whose first seven runs took an hour.

For Sussex, at Hove, in a match graced not only by two Kippax hundreds but by an appearance by another famous flyer, Amy Johnson, and copious quantities of golden wattle, Maurice Tate had Jackson caught at slip early in each innings, but not before he had given the crowd a good laugh by falling flat on his back as he made a lusty stroke to leg. His outfielding caught the eye here as well.

At Folkestone against an England XI, Archie had to prevent a hat-trick after Kippax had fallen first ball. This he did, and the five runs he needed for his thousand for the season soon came. His innings of 78 was full of beautiful leg-glides and cover-drives, and was happily completed on his twenty-first birthday. His progress was interrupted only by a blow to the abdomen from the lofty Maurice Allom which forced him to leave the field (Allom was bowling fast enough to break McCabe's middle stump). Archie Jackson had perceptive onlookers wondering why he had not been one of the season's consistent major successes. Doctors were to supply one of the explanations soon enough.

And so, after the farewell dinner given by MCC, the tourists travelled north for their last match in England, at Scarborough, where a large crab was found under the pitch covers at the start of the day. Archie Jackson made 24 "pretty" runs before being bowled by a ball which pitched leg and took off, delivered by the grand and cagey old hero Wilfred Rhodes, who, with his 53rd birthday imminent, was playing his last first-class match. With drizzle and murky light now coming as no surprise, the Australians drew the match, and thoughts finally turned to home.

Jackson pursued the sightseeing he had promised himself all along, and in the last week of September he wrote a farewell note to a young Hampshire farmer, Harry Mills, who had befriended him and Don Bradman:

> Five of our chaps left yesterday morning and only Hurwood and I are left at the Midland Grand. We visited the East End on Thursday last and enjoyed ourselves immensely. When you have the same experience you are going to enjoy it too. Well, Harry, as I will not see you again I do want to thank you for your many kindnesses and hope to see you again in 1934.

He had made 1097 runs, average 34.28, with that solitary century; was fifth in the Australian averages and aggregates; had both disappointed and delighted; and had earned £600 exclusive of the 30 shillings a week for incidental expenses.

Wealthy Australian soap manufacturer Arthur Whitelaw's £1000 token of admiration to Don Bradman set the world champion batsman apart—as if his record-breaking aggregate had not already done so. England's applause, as Geoffrey Tebbutt noted, had been ready for Jackson: "Bradman got it, and, I fear, that which was the due of some others as well!"

A tour diary kept by Alec Hurwood, which surfaced recently, revealed more about young Archie's tour experiences: Following the first day's play in the Lord's Test the pair walked around London, totting up eight miles by the Queenslander's estimate. During the Nottinghamshire match Hurwood and Jackson played billiards as guests of Lord Belper until late at night, after the other Australian players had all left. They had to be driven back to the hotel by His Lordship's chauffeur. It was noted that Archie played tennis at every opportunity, with Hurwood and Grimmett, and with Bradman whenever within range of his friend Harry Mills's court. On Saturday, July 12, it's recorded that Archie and Hurwood and Grimmett dined with Miss Somerville and the Misses Morrison in Leeds. In late July, when Archie Jackson made his sole tour century against Somerset, his partner Don Bradman was actually barracked. One can only assume that the spectators had downed too much cider that day. And in the final days of the tour Jackson and Hurwood ventured into London's East End, sampled three pubs, and gazed at the low life all around. (Another member of the tour party revealed to the author half-a-century later that he offered to take Archie Jackson to a house of ill fame with the intention of "breaking him in", but the youngster took fright and backed out at the last minute.) On a much higher plane, he had dined with Alec Hurwood and Bert Oldfield at the RAC Club in Pall Mall.

Archie was one of the small group of players who left England a few days after the rest of the team. The stragglers crossed Europe by rail and, on October 3, 1930, met up with the others aboard RMS Oronsay in Toulon, where the harbour was ominously full of warships. (This 20,000-ton vessel was sunk by a torpedo in October 1940, a tragic sacrifice to war, as also was the *Orford*, the ship which had taken the Australians to England months earlier.)

CHAPTER EIGHT

Flashes of Sunlight

Not for Archie Jackson the tumultuous homecoming. Having reached Melbourne, he said, "I was breaking my neck to be home and to see my cobbers."

So he flew on ahead of the team, and was missing when the crowds, reporters and reception party massed at Central Station on the official day of the team's arrival in Sydney. (He later politely apologised for any embarrassment he may inadvertently have caused.) Meanwhile, Don Bradman had been feted across Australia as he was escorted on a triumphal passage home to family and local friends.

Archie's mother was out shopping when he reached the house in Wrights Road, overlooking Five Dock Bay. But the unheralded reunion soon transpired, and he had a busy time keeping up with the questions and asking his own. He spent the Saturday calling on friends, and loosened up with a few games of tennis.

The local Press finally caught up with him, and saw him as being "in perfect health, as boyish and modest as ever". It had been a treat, he said, to play under Woodfull's captaincy. The skipper had been popular with players and opponents alike. Grimmett was the best slow bowler in the world, without question. But he sympathised with Alec Hurwood, who had shared a room with Archie through most of the tour. He was dreadfully unlucky.

"At no time did Hurwood bowl badly, but he just could not get wickets. Nobody could have been more popular. No matter what his success or failure, he always had a smile." (Hurwood was to play two Tests against West Indies during the next summer, taking 11 wickets cheaply then disappearing from Test cricket because of business interests.)

Jackson mentioned having had several tempting offers to play cricket in England, one in the Lancashire League and one with the county itself, the terms being a large lump sum, £10 a week (several times the basic wage of that period), and employment in a solicitor's office. But he had at least one reason for refusing: "The taxes are too heavy over there. But I am terribly keen to make the trip in 1934. I think that if I missed it I would be inclined to pack my bag and go all the same."

A West Indies side toured Australia during that summer of 1930-31, and Archie Jackson, with that admirable 73 at The Oval in the final Test having restored him to favour, must still have felt a need to prove his claims for inclusion in the forthcoming Test matches.

In Ryder's testimonial match at the MCG he failed twice for

the triumphant touring team against The Rest; but for New South Wales against the West Indians he made a pedigree 62 in the second innings, having been restored as opening batsman. It was a match set apart by the astonishing hitting of Learie Constantine, who launched some massive sixes off legspinner Hugh Chilvers and Archie's old mate Bill Hunt: one landed halfway up the Hill, another onto the Hill stand roof and into the Showground next door, and another way up onto the roof of the Sheridan Stand. (Chilvers used to challenge Archie to a quaint duel on long, boring interstate rail journeys. He would play the mouth-organ faster and faster to Archie's tap-dancing, each trying to outpace and exhaust the other.)

The pitches that season of 1930-31 turned out to be much too slow for the West Indies attack of Constantine, Griffith and Francis, and in the Test matches Constantine also failed disastrously with the bat. The tourists were crushed in the first four Tests, but, after M.A. Noble and "Chappie" Dwyer had influenced the preparation of the pitch at Sydney for the fifth contest, they won their first Test against Australia, with Frank Martin and the great George Headley, both Jamaicans, scoring hundreds, and the fast battery taking advantage of a rain-soaked pitch—a near-miraculous reversal.

By then Archie Jackson had lost his place after three failures at Sydney, Brisbane and Melbourne. In this fifth Test he came in as runner for an injured batsman on the final afternoon. It was to be the last time he set foot on the field in first-class cricket.

Outside the Test matches he had been quite successful, and he was certainly no failure in the first Test, at Adelaide, a ground of happy memories for him. Here, in the first-ever Australia-West Indies match, he (70 not out) and Ponsford (92 not out) hit the 170 needed for victory without being separated—after Kippax had proudly made the maiden century of the series in the first innings. Umpire Hele recalled: "As they walked out together, Jackson said to Ponsford, 'I see the skipper (Woodfull) is padded up. We won't give him a hit!'"

Ponsford, Woodfull and Bradman dominated the rest of the rubber, and Jackson, being favoured to Woodfull as opener until the fourth Test, had to stomach three successive failures before the selectors' axe inevitably fell.

He had been forced to leave the field through illness on the third day of the Brisbane Test, and missed the State match with Victoria immediately following.

His reappearance for the fourth Test, at Melbourne—a two-day affair in which he took four catches and Constantine dismissed him for 15—was his final big match. He was too sick to play for New South Wales against the tourists a week later, and was relegated to 12th man for the final Test match.

The only other performances he had to look back on with pleasure that season were a remarkable and splendid 166 as part of a record 334 stand with Bradman in the Shield match at Adelaide (when Bill Hunt bowled very effectively for New South Wales), and an earlier 53 at Brisbane in a match of gargantuan scoring, Cecil Thompson topping it off with 275 not out, a Queensland record.

And it was here in Brisbane that Archie met and fell for Phyllis (known as Phyl) Thomas. Frank Gough, the Queensland all-rounder, introduced them at a tennis party over the weekend. Phyl was only eighteen, and, having been trained in ballet, had found success in Sydney with an adagio dance act with her brother Ray. Barely five feet tall, she had the gaiety and sparkle that matched Archie's temperament perfectly. She loved cricket, attributing her enthusiasm to her mother. Mrs Thomas, who, as a girl in Bendigo, had lived next door to Harry Trott, the Australian Test captain of 1890s vintage, had always been keen on the game, and for a number of years she helped prepare the players' teas at Windsor Park, where Northern Suburbs played. So Brisbane now unexpectedly lured Archie Jackson with a romantic appeal.

He was now working at Anthony Horderns, and drawing large crowds to the Sydney department store to watch him bat in the nets. He had made a little extra money by putting his name on Surridge bats, though it seems his addiction to an old favourite that refused to wear out prevented him from actually using one.

Bill Hunt kept that bat of Archie's and used to draw attention to a flaw along the inside edge—a split which, if hit, would surely cause several inches to fly off: "But he didn't edge 'em down the leg side. He might've got out in the slips occasionally, but his leg glances were perfect. Really perfect!"

The blade has a concave at the meat which tells of hundreds of accurate strokes, and the perished rubber grip resembles an aerial view of the Amazon delta, just to remind its handler that much time has passed since it was unwrapped and given its preparatory oiling. It is a rousing relic, later passed to the author by Archie's Hampshire farmer friend Harry Mills.

The stricken cricketer picked up in health sufficiently to take part in a "missionary" tour of North Queensland in March 1931 with an assembly of players led by Alan Kippax. Showing extraordinary stamina and application, Jackson exceeded Victor Trumper's "record" of 1046 runs by 163 and averaged 86.35. He came back nicely sun-tanned and apparently fit and well, even though it had been quite an arduous expedition.

They had travelled for almost a week just to reach their starting point—Cairns—sailing via Brisbane and Townsville, motoring through the thick subtropical country of the Atherton Tablelands, along one 12-mile stretch of road which, someone dazedly discovered, incorporated 602 bends. On Malanda's concrete wicket Jackson made 61.

This he followed with 158 (the last 50 in 10 minutes) and 51 not out (in eight minutes) at Cairns, delighting the capacity crowd and playing through showers of rain that could only have exacerbated his condition.

Runs were three-a-minute all through the tour, and the light-hearted cricket of Kippax, Bradman, McCabe, Jackson, Fairfax and Wendell Bill filled the collection boxes and provided a nett profit of £3000 which in due course bought some turf pitches and general improvements. The stars were paid 10 shillings a day against loss of salary, and all travelling and accommodation expenses.

From Cairns they moved on to Innisfail, the centre of the sugar industry, where the townsfolk were complaining of a dry summer. The night after the team left, ten inches of rain fell—a phenomenon which might well have added to their mystique.

More of Archie's letters survive from this period. One, written from Innisfail, is disarmingly frank:

Our tour up here has been most pleasant, though I dislike intensely our present abode. It's such a wet town and it makes you feel miserable. The rainfall per year is 140 inches, about 110 inches more than we receive in Sydney over the same period. It rains nine months a year, and the population comprises the most cosmopolitan crowd in Australia, so it's rotten!

Our first game against Eacham at Malanda was very funny. The grass was long and wet so that to score a boundary the ball had to be lifted. Anyway, they batted first and reached 141. Kippax sent the other chaps in to keep their wickets intact so as we could bat in the afternoon. However, before long four were down for 15.

Then Fairfax went in (you know—the strong man!) to stop the rot. The first ball hit him on the gloves and he got one run. When he got up the other end the bowler hit him on the pad and he was given out. He certainly did perform, and spent the rest of the day plastering butter on the bruise. Kippax 32, Bradman 34 and myself 61, managed to evade defeat. The next match against Cairns was high-scoring. Bradman scored 103 and 90 and I got 158 and 50 n.o.

Last night a dance was held in our honour and the entire town turned out. We were kicked all over the body. It was so rough that Alan Fairfax reckoned he scored the final try just on time!

A sidelight of the match at Malanda was Jackson's planting of a tree to mark the team's visit. A leaf from the tree was later sent to Phyl, who placed it in a small scrapbook, where it remained a sweet link with a merry cricket tour long ago.

A seven-hour train journey had the players in Townsville for two two-day matches, the second, against a North Queensland representative XI, seeing four centuries from the New South

Wales side—Jackson 172. Then, after traversing more jungle, canefields and banana plantations, they played on Ayr's new turf pitch, where Bradman made the match his own, scoring 107 and taking 6 for 23 with leg-spin.

Another frenzied welcome at Bowen turned to delight in another massacre by the touring players. This time McCabe, Kippax and Jackson made hundreds.

They travelled overnight to Mackay and ran into more heavy rain, then left at 4.30 in the morning for another long, tiring haul to Rockhampton and, at last, three days of freedom, most of which was spent at the beach. They were still nineteen days from Brisbane, the last stop. Bradman had the misfortune—or perhaps merciful fortune—to sprain his ankle (not for the last time) in a hole at mid-on during the Rockhampton match, and had to remain behind.

As recorded by Philip Derriman, Archie batted against future Queensland premier Jack Pizzey in the Bundaberg match in April, and was suspicious of his slow left-arm deliveries. He turned to the young wicketkeeper (a future great) Don Tallon and asked if the bowler had a wrong-'un. Tallon, with surprising candour, replied that he hadn't. Jackson then played him with ease.

The fireworks continued at Gympie, where McCabe belted 173, including 40 off one over. By the time they reached Ipswich most of them were exhausted, and Archie Jackson poured it all out in another letter to Bill Hunt:

> Our tour of Nth Queensland has now concluded, and thank
> goodness! It has been rather a bore from start to finish,
> particularly as we had to attend so many dinners, socials,

BON VOYAGE: In the company of captain Bill Woodfull (far left), Bill Ponsford (SECOND FROM LEFT) and Alan Fairfax (SECOND FROM RIGHT), Archie (FAR RIGHT) enjoys the journey to England for the 1930 Ashes aboard Orford. It was a dream come true for Archie, but tough times awaited him in the months ahead.

↑ **COVER STAR:** Don Bradman (left) and Archie Jackson were as richly promising a pair of batsmen as ever excited a cricket nation at the same time. How could anyone have foreseen their contrasting destinies?

→ **MISSING OUT:** Archie is caught for 24 by future English Test batsman Cyril Walters in the Australians' match against Worcestershire in early May, 1930. In what became the story of the tour, Don Bradman strode to the crease in Jackson's wake and stroked a double-century at almost a run a ball.

↑ **NSW CONNECTION:** Archie (RIGHT) is joined for a portrait by fellow 1930 Ashes tourists Don Bradman (LEFT) and Alan Fairfax (MIDDLE), the latter praised by Bradman as the country's best all-rounder at that point.

← OPENING UP: Striding out onto Headingley with his captain Bill Woodfull for the third Test of the 1930 Ashes series, Archie Jackson was soon heading back to the pavilion with only one run to his name. Jackson then watched on as Australia's next man, Don Bradman, compiled 334—his highest score in Tests.

↑ **AT LAST:** Jackson drives for his long-awaited first century on English soil, in the Australians' match against Somerset at Taunton. 'The sun had thawed him out.'

↑ **CLEAN STROKE:** Archie plays the ball to leg for the sake of a photographer. Early observers of the slender and athletic Jackson's batting felt he had all the comely movement and keenness of eye of another of Sydney's Gods of Cricket, Victor Trumper.

← **CONTRAST:** Archie was a picture of relaxed elegance when playing the cover drive. That style provided an interesting counterpoint to life in Balmain, where, his friend Bill Hunt said, locals "spread coal dust on their bread."

↑ **BATTLING ON:** Bill Woodfull (LEFT), Australia's captain, takes Archie Jackson to open with him against Lancashire at Old Trafford, during the 1930 trip. The 20-year-old made 52 in two hours.

↑ **BAD LUCK:** Archie Jackson suffers a bad omen on his way out to bat at Bristol in August, 1930, which finished in a thrilling tie after openers Jackson and McCabe had made half of the Australians' requirement of only 118.

← **TWO COLTS:** Archie with Don Bradman, the batsman to whom he was favourably compared.

↑ **POISE:** With all the balance of a ballet dancer, Jackson swings a ball from Peebles away during the Oval Test, which would be Archie's last on English soil.

← **AGONY:** Never one to shirk a hostile spell of fast bowling, Archie was as brave on the field as he was stoic off it. Here, in the Oval Test of 1930, he feels the wrath of Harold Larwood, the man Jackson dubbed "The Red Devil".

↓ **COUNTER-ATTACK:** Archie hooks at The Oval during the 1930 Ashes series.

↑ **FINE FETTLE:** Having struggled with illness and damp pitches on the 1930 England tour, Archie Jackson fired in the Oval Test, scoring 73 in Australia's mammoth first innings of 695. Below Archie demonstrates his famed late cut.

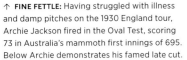

ARCHIE JACKSON

↑ **FAMILY TIES:** In November 1930, fresh from his maiden Ashes tour, Archie is more comfortable posing with his mother Margaret and sister Peggie. Mr and Mrs Jackson maintained a quiet pride in the rapid progress of their only boy.

SOCIAL ENGAGEMENTS: Affable Archie was nobody's idea of a ladies man, but when good health allowed him onto the social circuit during the 1930 Ashes tour (ABOVE), he always mixed well. On the horizon was a short and sadly doomed romance with ballet dancer Phyllis Thomas, pictured below with her brother Ray.

WITH BEST WISHES: A proud and modest cricketer, Archie sent the memento at left to a friend in England. Whether Australia pickd him or not, Archie was determined to return to England in 1934.

← **NAMES AND FACES:** Ready with a smile, Archie (LEFT) greets his teammate Bert Oldfield in March, 1930. The pair shared in the highs and lows of life; Oldfield was a fellow Ashes tourist of Archie's in 1930, but barely three years later the wicketkeeper was among the pall-bearers carrying a beloved teammate to his final resting place.

CALYPSO SUMMER: Australia v West Indies, Sydney, February 1931. Archie Jackson was 12th man for this Test. Back row, L-R: R.K. Oxenham, J.E.D. Sealy, W.H. Ponsford, G.A. Headley, A.A. Jackson, H.C. Griffith, K.E. Rigg, G.N. Francis. Middle row, L-R: S.J. McCabe, I. Barrow, A.G. Fairfax, O.C. Scott, H. Ironmonger, C.A. Roach, W.A.S. Oldfield, E.L. Bartlett. Front row, L-R: H Armstrong (Umpire), D.G. Bradman, F.R. Martin, A.F. Kippax, C.G. Grant (West Indies Captain), W.M. Woodfull (Australian Captain), L.S. Birkett, C.V. Grimmett, L.N. Constantine, W.G. French (Umpire).

REUNION: In April 1932, having been forced by his illness to give up the strenuous demands of big cricket, Archie Jackson (centre) is reunited with teammates Don Bradman (right) and Jack Fingleton.

DYING DAYS: Putting on a brave face, Archie Jackson posed for the camera at Calvary Hospital, Adelaide, in 1932, as his battle against insidious disease continued.

DAY OF MOURNING: A *Sydney Mail* photograph from February 22, 1933: "A large crowd witnessed the departure of the funeral from the former international's old home, and thousands attended the Field of Mars, where Archie Jackson was laid to rest."

A SPORTING TRAGEDY: Archie Jackson's coffin is carried to its final resting place in the Field of Mars Cemetery, in the Sydney suburb of Ryde, by pall-bearers (from right) Bill Woodfull, Vic Richardson, Bill Ponsford and Don Bradman. Jackson's NSW skipper Alan Kippax replaced Stan McCabe at the graveside when he became ill, a feeling shared by a nation in mourning for its batting genius.

FINAL TRIBUTE: As Australians reeled from the shock of Archie Jackson's death, tributes flowed from all corners of the globe. The great batsman's headstone spoke most succinctly of his life: "He played the game."

VISITING FRIENDS: Former NSW and Australian cricketer Bill Hunt attends to his old pal's grave, 40 years on from Archie's death. In a tribute to his friend, Hunt had worn a pair of Archie's trousers during his sole Test against South Africa in January, 1932.

FAMILY HEIRLOOM: Archie's youngest sister Jeanie with her brother's Australian blazer, outside her home in 1972. In his lifetime, Archie spoilt his little sister more with each passing year.

THE PASSING OF TIME: Archie's fiancée Phyl (née Thomas) later in life. When she first met Archie as an 18-year-old, she had the gaiety and sparkle that matched Archie's temperament perfectly.

dances, etc, and in every case finance was the ideal. I would never make this trip again unless I was guaranteed £100, and that's not enough!

With all due modesty, I have had a most successful tour and have scored 1100 runs average 93.00, with six centuries. I am, of course, heading both aggregate and average, and may just possibly scrape together another century before the tour definitely concludes.

I was extremely disappointed at the failure of Balmain in the last two rounds, but I'm sure they will do much better next year.

You certainly had a particularly pleasant season, and you surely must be given a chance against the Sth Africans. If, because of the exchange, they cannot fulfil their itinerary in Australia, it is quite possible that we may go to Africa. How would you like the trip, Bill? It would certainly be a great one from every point of view, and if you were one of the tourists it would make you a star.

What have you to tell me that is so interesting regarding the girl opposite? Have you arranged our wedding, or merely fixed our engagement? However I am still interested. After all it is most likely worth exploring.

Well, Bill, I must close now, but would like to tell you that Alan Fairfax stated he is dying to meet Balmain next season just for the satisfaction of cracking you over the fence a few times. Still, I don't think he could crack me!

It was a happy, hopeful, teasing letter from a man full of the joys of living.

CHAPTER NINE

Summer Ends

Archie kept in trim during the 1931 winter with plenty of golf and tennis, which also helped keep his mind off the economic crisis. The Government Savings Bank had frozen depositors' funds, and so tight was the situation that he had to decline the offer of his friend Harry Mills to send a gift of a wireless from England because of the excise duty of £15 that would have been payable in Sydney.

Harry sent the set all the same, and in the letter of thanks Archie remarked on the mildness of the Australian winter: "It is to be hoped that summer proves just as mild. Sometimes we get some hellish heatwaves that make a fellow pine for the cold of England, though people are never satisfied, are they?"

His recurring sickness, still only at the nuisance level and not yet diagnosed as anything critical, had lapsed once more into inertia as the 1931-32 cricket season opened, although at least one friend was struck by the profusion of medicine bottles in Archie's room.

He made a lot of runs on a country tour with Alan Kippax's side, and when he played a showpiece innings of 183 for Balmain—his highest ever—against Gordon, he and his supporters had every hope and expectation that he would feature prominently for State and country against the visiting South Africans.

He was selected for the opening Sheffield Shield match of the season and travelled with the team to Brisbane, but having just recovered from a bout of influenza he had the misfortune to be caught in a rain-squall while crossing the Hawkesbury River, and his chest ailment was activated.

On Friday morning, November 6, 1931, Phyl sat with her lunch-box and clapped with the crowd as the New South Wales players took the field at the Gabba. Then she noticed that Archie wasn't among them. While she was wondering what could possibly have happened to him, Alan Fairfax came over and broke the news that Archie had coughed up blood, collapsed and been rushed to hospital. Would she please get some pyjamas for him?

It was a dreadful shock, and both teams were plunged into deep gloom when the New South Wales manager gave them the news.

The emergency dealt with, a sensational match ensued: later in the day Eddie Gilbert, the diminutive Aboriginal, bowling with furious speed and bounce, dismissed Don Bradman for a duck, and Alan Kippax suffered a jagged cut on the temple after mis-hooking "Pud" Thurlow (and finished up in the next hospital bed to Archie's, according to *Australian Cricketer* magazine). Stan McCabe played what he always considered the innings of his life (and there were several classics to choose from), rising from his team's desperate plight to score an undefeated 229, while Jackson's replacement, Jack Fingleton, made a dour 93.

Archie Jackson, who, to judge from a later letter, believed himself to be a flu victim, was discharged from hospital after five days and returned to Sydney with the team. Within a week, at the instigation of the Board of Control, he was installed in Bodington Sanitorium at Wentworth Falls, in the Blue Mountains. It was announced that he would not be playing cricket in the foreseeable future.

Bill Hunt and his fiancée Ann made the journey to see him at every opportunity, and took him on the bus into Springwood for tea—as much as anything to release him from the coughing and spitting all around him.

He was frustrated beyond description. He wanted letters from friends, yet those same letters lured his spirit down to the lowlands that he loved. He needed the companionship of his mates and parents and of Phyl.

After a few months in the institution, he felt a need to find an abode of his own. So he took a cottage, "Tranmere", in The Mall at Leura, and there sister Peggie joined him for the remainder of the summer and through the winter of 1932.

In April he broke away briefly to Sydney and called in on "Johnnie" Moyes, then sports editor of *The Sun*. Moyes wrote hopefully: "I have not seen him since his return from Brisbane, stricken with the illness that caused his withdrawal from cricket. The change was remarkable. Then he looked the sick man that he was. Now he has about him an air of health, activity, and optimism. Will he play again next season? Time alone will tell, but the delightful batsman is full of hope."

It so happened that Don Bradman and Jack Fingleton walked in moments later, and Moyes speculated on the possibility of the three of them heading the New South Wales batting line-up before long.

Several other times Jackson slipped away from his mountain retreat and appeared without warning on the doorstep at home or at Bill Hunt's place. His parents were understanding, but Mr Hunt senior, who cherished him as would a father, withheld his pleasure at seeing him and adopted what he felt was the only fit stance: "Go back to Leura, Archie. We don't want to see you down here till you're well again. Come back when you're cured and you'll be as welcome as the day is long."

In January, Bill Hunt received his Test invitation, at the bottom of which was a postscript from W.C. Bull to the effect that Dr Collins had recently examined Archie and found him to be making "excellent progress".

In a letter to Harry Mills in May, Archie stated his aims clearly enough:

> I should dearly love to play against the Englishmen next season, so can only hope for the best. I've quite decided on another visit to England in 1934, whether as a member of the Aust. XI or not so... less than two years hence too! Perhaps I'll qualify for a county—who knows! I would like to spend a few years in England. What a time we'd have. By that time I would be nearly 25 years of age.. . at all events old enough to paint dear old London red.

Clarifying his situation, he told his old friend about an alarming interlude:

> I had a severe breakdown, contracted pleurisy, and for a few weeks my life was in jeopardy. However I managed to pull through and am depending on my present sedentary existence to completely restore me to my usual state of health.

At the time of writing it was "frightfully cold", and he was spending the greater part of each day curled up in front of the fire reading.

He went on to express concern for Alan Fairfax, who was having hardly any success with Accrington in the Lancashire League, and lamented his own wicked luck in having to miss the tour by Arthur Mailey's side through Canada and America (Don and Jessie Bradman's honeymoon tour): "Still, it is probably for the best, and after all I'll see America even if I have to wait for a few years."

Turning to the dismissal of the Lang State Government as the Depression bit, he was inclined towards a feeling of relief: "Lang has created a good deal of turmoil and strife, and almost any change must be for the best. Stevens, the new leader, is a fine type of man and has already gained the confidence of the people."

Among more mundane matters he asked Harry to send him a couple of cheap grey hats, size 6g: "Australian hats have a larger brim than the English, and as I have the brim down I look like a cowboy."

It so happens that Archie and Don Bradman briefly feature in a film made by Percy Fender during the 1928-29 tour of Australia. Awaiting a train at a bush railway junction, they are both wearing hats with wide brims. They smile self-consciously in the direction of the Englishman's camera, revealing young Bradman's uneven teeth (he was to undergo major dental surgery four years later, just before the Bodyline series began).

In part-exchange for the hoped-for narrow-brimmed hat. Archie was going to send his Hampshire friend Harry a bat: "It was used twice against the Englishmen in Tests and three times against the West Indies as well as a few State games, so it's quite a warrior."

A later letter, in August, revealed that Archie planned to sail for England in April 1933: "but I can't say anything further at the moment."

He was still concerned about the weather, which had been unusually cold, but was looking forward to some fun in the snow which lay thick over the mountains.

Correspondence between the New South Wales Cricket Association, Archie and various doctors, which came to light as recently as 1983, reveals the tug of war between the authorities, who believed the sanatorium was the only place for the sick batsman, and the young cricketer himself, who was desperate to get away. "I find it almost impossible to consume my food with fellow patients," he wrote plaintively. He had "implicit confidence" in Dr McIntosh at Leura. He was "facing my position more squarely by entering his supervision and have absolute faith in the knowledge that my cure will be complete."

He considered the attitude of Dr Collins, the Board's medical advisor, "unfair and unjust": "He is not infallible and I shall certainly prove him wrong". Dr Collins wanted him to stay at Bodington for a further three months.

"Do be patient, Archie," wrote the white-bearded A.W. Green, a NSWCA committee member, who pointed out that to have the disease under control was one thing; but it could be subject to "re-infection".

In another letter, to Bill Hunt, Archie claimed that Dr McIntosh had told him he was out of danger, and should be able to play against England in the 1932-33 series. His greatest fear was of "contracting the germ once again" while in the sanatorium.

The risk that he would forfeit the financial support of the NSWCA was ever present, though a letter reveals that, having left Bodington, he was granted £3.3.0 a week, for which he expressed profuse gratitude. He also told Green that he now weighed 10st 8lb, 3lb up on his weight upon arrival.

In July 1932, NSWCA secretary Harold Heydon wrote to Archie in Calvary Hospital, Adelaide, asking about his financial situation. The Association were debating whether to continue with the grant. Heydon also wrote to Dr McIntosh, who explained that Archie had gone to Adelaide, with his "permission", for treatment to his skin condition, which had worsened. Dr McIntosh assured the committee that he felt Archie was "playing the game".

Heydon's next piece of news came via a somewhat mystical telegram from Archie in Adelaide. "Your letter delayed," it read. Then: "Had five hundred and fifty (pounds) six months ago, now three hundred and ninety. Letter following."

He wrote that his health was "really splendid", and he expected to participate in at least a few first-class matches next season. Umpire George Hele had been to see him at the hospital in Hutt Street, as had some of the South Australia players, the main topic of conversation being whether Australia would retain the Ashes against Jardine's England team. He had an occasional hit in the nets, and renewed other friendships, one being with Minnie Rosman, an elderly spinster who had been his "South Australian mother".

Then came a letter which must have struck the NSWCA committee like a thunderbolt. It was a confidential report from a physician in Adelaide, who stated that Archie Jackson, while in Calvary Hospital, "expectorated a small quantity of blood. The examination of his sputum showed very numerous tubercle bacilli". Clinical examination showed that he had "pneumonary tuberculosis with fairly extensive involvement of the lungs".

The doctor at Leura still seemed satisfied with his progress, and Archie began to think in terms of returning to civilisation. But it needed time—plenty of time. He was impatient. He wanted to be with Phyl again. So he formulated the plan to live in Brisbane, where the hotter climate, in his misguided opinion, would promote his restoration.

As a new summer dawned he released himself from his mountain exile and took up the threads of living once more.

Moving up the latitudes to Brisbane, he spent some time at Brookstead, 140 miles west of Brisbane and drought-stricken. In a letter to Harold Heydon he explained that his health was "perfectly good" and that the northern clime seemed to be beneficial as his weight was now 10st 10lbs. A few days later the NSWCA wrote to him to say that his allowance would cease in a fortnight. He wrote expressing his thanks and saying that he had been offered a position in Queensland.

Meanwhile, the Adelaide physician had been asked to report on Archie's condition yet again. His view was brighter this time, though he warned that he could not play serious cricket without "very harmful results following". He had agreed to the move to Queensland so long as he took great care of himself and returned to the Blue Mountains for the summer.

Finally came Archie's reassurance, in a letter of thanks to A.W. Green of the NSWCA, that he expected to regain his health completely while up north, but would return one day to his home State and "again don the blue cap".

Countless hopes and prayers were with him as he whitened his cricket boots again. Eric Barbour summed it up in *The Sydney Mail*, recalling Jackson's "body blows from Tate and Larwood that might well have daunted a Carnera [giant Italian boxer]". He wrote: "We all hope that the gallant pluck that carried Archie through this searching test will help him to throw off his present illness, and that we shall soon see him resume the place in the Australian XI that he has so honestly won."

The incredible fact is that, having gone to Brisbane, he offered his services to Northern Suburbs and proceeded—though fearfully short of breath—to make a staggering number of runs. It is worth recounting his full performances on a country tour and in Brisbane in 1932-33: 104, 60, 100, 53 not out, 56 not out, 66 not out, 37, 17, 155 (Queensland trial match), 105 not out, 14, 124 not out, and 77. Genius was prevailing.

His seven innings for Northern Suburbs drew record crowds, and left him with an average of 159.66 after batting against such quality opponents as Eddie Gilbert, Ron Oxenham, Percy

Hornibrook, "Pud" Thurlow and Herb Gamble.

It was eye-opening, but some old club cricketers in Brisbane later remembered how it was cutting away his life. One, Tom O'Shea, of the Valley club, off whom Jackson scored his last century, recalled it as "a delightful, pathetic innings. Delightful in his strokemaking against our weak attack but pathetic to witness his suffering. I vividly recall his state of exhaustion when he had to hurry between wickets. He'd spar for time by bending down to adjust his pads. Goodness knows how many his innings was worth had he been able to run for all available runs."

Future Test umpire Col Hoy graphically recalled the desperate nature of the situation. As a youngster he had watched Archie batting for Norths, and saw him retire from the crease in some distress. In Ian Diehm's superb Queensland cricket history, *Green Hills to the Gabba*, he records Hoy's vivid recollection: "He had to retire coughing and spitting up. Archie went into the dressing-room in the little grandstand and was lying on a bench. He raised his head as I walked in. He looked up and said 'What's the matter, kiddo?' 'Can I have your autograph?' I asked. 'Yes, son. Will you take my pads off please?' I did, and he said 'Thanks.' Next minute, Dr Alex Mayes came in and showed me out. Archie was coughing up black stuff—real yukkie. Not long after, Archie Jackson died and I just threw myself on my bed and sobbed my heart out."

Some thought that Archie should have been banned from playing cricket, so patently obvious was the strain on his body. The exertion was the last thing his failing lungs needed. These were times when tuberculosis was largely incurable, with fatal consequences. The young man's optimism and determination were truly extraordinary.

Alan McGilvray recalled how, in one of Archie's last innings in Sydney grade cricket, the fielding side had faced the agonising dilemma of whether to run-out the gasping out-of-breath Jackson to save him further exhaustion, or to spare him so that his obsessive but self-destructive love of batting could continue to be gratified: a harrowing choice of mercies.

Having emigrated north seemingly impulsively, he boarded with another very fine young New South Wales batsman, Maitland-born Charlie "Cassie" Andrews, who had also moved north (and already knew young Phyl). He gave Andrews a bat which was greatly cherished. Soon Archie moved in at the home of Phyl's parents in Old Sandgate Road, Clayfield. On October 2, he wrote to Bill Hunt (Count) to apologise:

> Terribly sorry I was unable to get over to the 'Main and say Au Revoir to you prior to my departure to Brisbane, but was so busy was unable to do so. Know you will forgive me.
>
> Started grade cricket yesterday, Count, and on a wet wicket too. Nth Suburbs played Toombul. We had first knock and scored 101 of which I contributed 56 not out. Toombul have lost nine for 87, so the position is extremely interesting...
>
> A crowd of over 2000 watched the game—a record for Brisbane pennant cricket. Like Noodles Fairfax, my personality is magnetic—oh yeh? Bought a car the other day, Bill—a Chrysler Roadster, and quite a good job too. Paid £165 cash for it, but believe me it's worth it. So, m'lud, when you come north with the State team I'll only charge you a bob a mile. How does that suit you, eh?
>
> Start in the Brisbane Sports Depot tomorrow. Coach in the afternoon, and I think I'll be contributing weekly articles to the

Daily Mail. The Brisbane public will shortly be wondering who
this Bill Hunt is.

By the way, Count, you might send up the Walter Hammond
bat if you have no further use for it. Should imagine it is still
good for a few more hundreds.

He proceeded, in fact, to work as advisory sales assistant
at Johnson's Sports Depot in Queen Street, Brisbane (also
sponsoring their brand of cricket boot), to act as assistant coach
to the QCA, and to write regularly for the *Daily Mail*.

He and Phyl spent a lot of time together, and from the wings
of the theatre he often watched her performance. When she
attracted prolonged applause one evening he chuckled: "For a
moment I thought it was me out there!"

He spent more time reading, and in December started
Lowell Thomas's *With Lawrence in Arabia* (now safe in the
author's library thanks to the generosity of the Jackson family).

There was a sublime longing throughout the nation for
him to return to big cricket, and only the selectors' sense of
responsibility kept him out. The Press clamoured for his
inclusion in the exploratory Australian XIs that played Jardine's
1932-33 MCC team at Perth and Melbourne, for although it
had been decided that he was as yet ineligible for Queensland,
a longish innings against Larwood, Voce, Bowes, Allen and
company could have warranted a return to the Test side.

But it was reported in mid-November that he was thought
unlikely to be able to take the strain of a four-day match, and
therefore had not been considered. E.A. Shaw, Queensland's
manager, was certain that he hadn't the strength to endure
a gruelling first-class match. Archie, of course, felt otherwise.

He wrote to a friend in England that he felt strong and was certain he would be fit enough to play, "but one never knows what is lurking around the corner".

To Harry Mills, his Hampshire friend, he wrote on the last day of October 1932 that he had already made nearly 700 runs, but "unfortunately, though, I have violated the Board of Control rule re writing for the Press, so I don't suppose I'll be allowed to participate in the Tests this season. Still, old chap, the game must take second place to a man's living."

His plans had of necessity been modified already: "Oh, by the way, Harry, I'm a Queenslander these days. I came up here for health reasons and will probably stay for a season or two."

He was concerned at Queensland's poor showing against Victoria, but felt there was something he could do about it: "I am available against Victoria later in the year, so hope to strengthen the batting. You see, one has to reside in a State for three months before playing, and I've only been here about two months. Naturally, Harry, now that I'm residing in Queensland I will not be able to go to England in March next. However, I fully expect to get back into the Australian XI and visit England again in 1934. So, old chap, look out for me then."

His writings in The *Daily Mail* reflected acute insight and, predictably, some sensibility. He noted in the cricket of his adopted State "a most pronounced inferiority complex (that) will, unless eradicated, tend to retard the progress of Queensland cricket."

In a coaching article he wrote ruminatively that "the late-cut, perfectly executed, is the most delightful yet most dangerous stroke in the game."

Recalling his many country tours through both States "in an endeavour to unearth another Trumper or Turner", he turned his attention to the country lads who came to Brisbane for trials. Don Tallon, of Bundaberg, he thought, "may emulate the deeds with bat and gloves of Les Ames of Kent", and of Eddie Gilbert, the Aborigine: "having batted against him on three occasions, I have no hesitation in declaring his delivery fair and above suspicion." (His mate Bill Hunt thought otherwise.)

As the Ashes battle loomed he urged the inclusion of younger players, preferring Fleetwood-Smith ("the very man to rout the Englishmen") to Ironmonger, O'Reilly to Oxenham, and probably having more faith in Lonergan than in the recently battered Kippax. He felt Ponsford would be of more use to Australia batting down the order.

He was so inclined towards youth that he gave every impression that he considered 'Scarlet' Grimmett to be all but finished: "It has been gradually forced upon our senses that Grimmett is a back number, and is being carried in the team."

Grimmett, of course, lasted several years more, surviving a barren series now, but taking large bundles of wickets in England and South Africa. But Jackson was quite excited by a Queensland spinner named Jack Govan, who had some moments of glory, particularly when he bowled "unbowlable" Woodfull. "If Govan is ever selected to tour England with an Australian XI, he will realise that the reward for his perseverance is indeed great. Money cannot buy a trip home with an Australian XI, and the happy memories last for ever."

Soon he found himself in the strange position of watching from the Press-box as Alan Kippax made 179 for New South

Wales against Queensland, and, bold pupil, tendering advice: "He should continue to bat brilliantly, and not concentrate too much on defence"—perhaps less trite than it appeared.

In the same match Archie's old schoolmate Syd Hird also made a hundred, the merit of which was loyally drawn to the attention of the Australian selectors, although he later felt compelled to reproach Hird for his "unimpressive" leg-spin bowling.

Sometimes his claims were a shade extravagant. In listing four promising Brisbane cricketers he wrote: "These young players look better than Don Bradman did when he first strolled on the Sydney Cricket Ground, a novice of the willow, but today a potentate of the game."

Yet all he aimed to do was to encourage, encourage, encourage.

He raised his hands in horror at the thought of veterans Leo O'Connor and Cec Thompson returning to the Queensland side, and asserted that withdrawal from the Sheffield Shield competition would be a preferable course until suitable young blood could be found.

By the middle of January the Test series had reached fever pitch. England's Bodyline bowling attack had divided the country into one multitudinous, offended protest group on the one hand, and on the other a few who felt the tactics would not necessarily kill off the game of cricket and several participants with it.

Archie Jackson belonged to the minority, his indisposition making him seem like the retired old warrior, in his armchair, telling the novices how it should be done. It was general knowledge that he had never been short of courage himself, but although it can never be known just how he would have dealt with the hostile short-pitched leg-side attack, the fact remained that he was frustratingly unable to demonstrate his views in a practical way.

He was utterly sincere in his belief that Larwood and Voce could be handled and scored from. On his deathbed he told his friends repeatedly that the Australians simply needed to accelerate their footwork. For a time he actually nursed hopes that he might have an opportunity to prove his notion.

Nevertheless, his views were sought, and he felt obliged to air an opinion. True to himself as ever, he wrote what he believed. His criticism of certain players may have stung, but three weeks later it fell into perspective as it became apparent that the opinions were those of a young man whose lifeblood was draining rapidly away.

"Other writers have said that Ponsford and Fingleton have been battered unmercifully about the body. That is mostly their own fault... Fingleton, like Woodfull, is a flat-footed batsman ... Bradman and McCabe, on the other hand, have hardly felt the impact of leather on flesh, primarily because their movements are snappy enough to allow them to glide to the off side and allow the balls to fly harmlessly by... I have always believed, and still do, that Richardson is not a Test match player... For the sake of Australia's sporting traditions, may it be left to the cricketers themselves to furnish the only answer to the legitimate tactics employed by the Englishmen... It is my belief that Larwood would not intentionally hurt a fly." Very few people in Australia in January 1933 would have been prepared to accept that dismissive tailpiece.

On February 10, 1933 the fourth Test match began at the Gabba ground in Brisbane, but Archie Jackson was not there to see it. Early in the month he had collapsed after playing cricket, and was taken to Ingarfield Private Hospital. He had batted with a runner in most of his later innings, fellow New South Wales exile "Cassie" Andrews being his final escort.

With tuberculosis rife in both lungs, he was sinking before Phyl's helpless gaze. She witnessed at the closest quarters the fading of his summery skin tan and the emaciation that eroded his physique. Sensing they would never have the chance of marrying, but reflecting on the reality that doctors at times had been mistaken, they announced their betrothal a week after her twenty-first birthday. They did not marry, as claimed in Wisden.

Phyl, weeping inside, kept up her nightly and matinee ballet performances in the Minstrel Show at the Regent Theatre, and came faithfully to the hospital straight after the curtain, usually with her stage make-up sustaining facial cheer. She would reminisce, and find light subjects to touch upon, pretending that all would be well. Her beloved boy-man Archie, fighting exhaustion, losing weight, fading away, managed to muster a smile from time to time.

Back in Balmain unawareness suddenly turned to alarm as a "come quick" telegram arrived. Mrs Jackson set out on the long and testing train journey north, and Archie's father and family friends, the Walkers, followed. Bill Hunt flew to Brisbane with the celebrated aviator P.G. Taylor a week later. Archie, having suffered a severe haemorrhage, was in a very poor state when he arrived.

While that decisive Test match was played out in a heatwave, Bill Hunt read the newspaper reports to his dying friend while Australia tottered towards another defeat. "I want to get back, Bill," Archie gasped.

A number of players visited him, including Bill Woodfull, Bill Ponsford, Len Darling, Ernie Bromley, George Duckworth, Arthur Mailey, MCC manager 'Plum' Warner, and some of the England players. Of all Harold Larwood's many mementoes, one item—a slip of paper—remains more precious than any other: a telegram from Archie Jackson dated February 15. "Congratulations," it read. "magnificent bowling. Good luck all matches. Archie Jackson."

He was hardly ever alone in those last days. A local Methodist minister, H.M. Wheller, came to his bedside daily, and on his second-last visit he read him the 23rd Psalm, his favourite. They talked briefly and then prayed, and as the minister departed Archie raised his eyes and said, "Thank you. That has meant a great deal to me."

Later, when his mother came back into the room, he whispered that he was happy.

The relatives looked on helplessly as the flaxen-haired young man lay still, fighting weakly for breath. On the Wednesday afternoon he rallied slightly and wanted to know the Test score. He sank into a deep sleep.

Fifteen minutes after midnight on February 16, 1933, Archie Jackson's valiant fight for life ended. The mourning would last for years.

CHAPTER TEN

A Man Can
Only Fight

The unsuspecting Australian people, who had followed his exciting progress and placed so much hope on his delicate form, were stunned by the news of his death. Those closer to him had feared the worst for some time. To them the reality was harrowing, hardly diminishing as the months passed.

Johnnie Moyes, who remembered him as a 15-year-old at Chatswood Oval batting against Macartney and Kelleway with eye-catching aplomb, wrote that "all the disasters which have befallen our cricketers in the field are now as nothing compared with the loss to cricket of this great exponent of the game."

Moyes spoke for the nation. But the grief was at two levels, and to those who had known Archie Jackson intimately there seemed neither justification nor meaning in his fate. It led some to question their beliefs.

But it was one moment inevitable, the next a tragic truth. In hard proof, the flags at the Gabba were at half-mast and the players and umpires wore black arm-bands on the final day of the Test match, though some must still have felt that the pale, smiling face was looking out at them from the pavilion shadows. As a heroic backdrop to this tragedy, Eddie Paynter had got up from a sick-bed in a Brisbane hospital and made telling runs for the victorious Englishmen.

Alan Kippax, who was making daily broadcasts on the Tests, had the opportunity of paying his very personal tribute to his precious protege to both Australian and English radio audiences.

For a day the casket remained at the Thomas home, then on the Friday, at South Brisbane station, Phyl's brother and father and Bill Hunt assisted as pall-bearers, carrying their precious burden to the train past a silent assembly. In a kind of Viking glory, Archie Jackson's remains were conveyed back to Sydney in the same coach of the mail train that carried his parents and the solemn Test cricketers of Australia and England.

A large gathering awaited the train at Central station around seven on the Saturday morning, and as the cortege passed Gladesville Reserve, where a match was in progress, the cricketers broke off play to circle the pitch in bareheaded homage.

At the Jackson home in Wrights Road an enormous assemblage of people waited quietly outside the house and along the street, boys with bats and stumps limp in their hands, adults, some curious, some weeping openly or within.

A brief service was conducted in the home, Archie's parents and sisters, on whom he'd doted, in attendance, and then in mid-morning the mile-long cortege moved off for the Field of Mars Cemetery, through dense crowds which had begun to form hours earlier along Victoria Road and Lyons Road, three- or four-deep most of the way.

The scene at the cemetery was also Valentino-like in its fervour and confusion as the coffin, preceded by members of the Haberfield Lodge, to which Archie had belonged, was slowly borne to the graveside. The Rev. Sam McKibbin, formerly of Balmain Methodist Mission, had travelled especially from Singleton—this had been one of Archie's dying wishes—and he now delivered a touching address.

The pall-bearers who carried Archie to his final rest were all Test cricketers, his kinsmen until so recently: Bill Woodfull, Vic Richardson, Don Bradman, Bert Oldfield, Stan McCabe, and Bill Ponsford. Alan Kippax replaced McCabe at the graveside when he became ill.

The cemetery, next to the orchards where Archie scrumped apples as a boy, had never known such a sea of mourners. They came from miles around notwithstanding the long walk.

There were numerous cricketers, and representatives of all branches of sport, business and government, from Balmain, throughout the State, and from all over Australia. Rozelle Public School had paraded en masse and observed a silence, and the boys' wreath was accompanied by a letter of condolence which, with all the other cards and letters (and a cable from

Alan Fairfax, who now lived in England), filled an album three inches thick. This was but a symbol of the uttered sympathy, and took no account of the sorrow felt by a million anonymous citizens. Even the newsboys who sold papers at the Sydney Cricket Ground took up a collection and within minutes had thirty shillings for a wreath.

Anthony Horderns, no longer able to offer shoppers the entrancing batting displays by their young hero, set aside a special window as a memorial, with his portrait, stumps, a bat and wreath draped in velvet.

It was a time to reflect on past events and conversations. Eddie Shaw, who wrote for *The Telegraph* as "Third Man", could not forget Archie's fighting spirit. Only days before being rushed to hospital for the last time he had told Shaw that he felt the cards were stacked against him. "But, with a characteristic smile, he added: 'A man can only fight this thing out; if he wins it has been worthwhile; if he goes under, well, he at heart feels that what is to be will be'."

Test skipper Bill Woodfull, in making public his sorrow, remarked on Archie Jackson's "happy optimism" when he and some other players visited him in hospital.

Don Bradman, in a radio tribute, remembered how, four years earlier almost to the day, they had batted together against England at Adelaide in a vain effort to stave off defeat. He believed him to have been a batting genius. Years later, he recalled that his dear friend had not been a "positional" batsman who hit the ball in front of the wicket; "he relied more on touch and using the pace of the ball to glance and so on."

"Johnnie" Moyes wrote in Sydney's *Sun* newspaper:

"He flashed across the cricket skies like a meteor. We had not realised to the full the brilliancy of his art when suddenly he was gone, but he left cricket the richer for his brief sojourn. He left, too, memories that we will cherish of a truly great batsman and a splendid sportsman."

Balmain historian Cliff Winning later wrote: "He was one of the most lovable characters to ever don cricketing attire and was accepted by all who knew him as a gentleman by instinct, modest and retiring and one who practised the true culture of the mind, his thinking always being clear and clean and Christianlike." It truly was an immense loss.

At a memorial service held at Balmain Central Methodist Mission, England's tour manager 'Plum' Warner ascended the pulpit and delivered a touching address which was relayed by loudspeaker to the crowds outside and broadcast through 2BL. Bill Woodfull, Alan Kippax and Arthur Mailey also spoke.

The congregation sang *Jesu, Lover of My Soul*, a hymn so often sung by Archie to his own piano accompaniment. He had told his mother frequently "there is no hymn quite like this".

A letter written by Archie on January 23 and sent sea-mail reached Harry Mills in England almost a month after the world had learned of his passing. "England, to my way of thinking," he had written, "will win the Ashes in Brisbane."

He referred to Larwood as "a devastating whirlwind" and noted that "the Australian batsmen are beginning to squeal—certainly a rotten thing to say—but it's a fact creating a good deal of unnecessary trouble."

He explained his absence from the Queensland side: "It is too late in the season. I want to start off fresh next season...

I had another knock yesterday, the first for five weeks. I scored 77 in 94 minutes, so am still in pretty good form." That was to be his final innings.

On September 3, as the result of a public subscription, a red granite headstone, designed by former Test cricketer Tommy Andrews, who was a monumental mason, was unveiled by the New South Wales premier B.S.B. Stevens. He addressed a very large company of people, Phyl among them, and said that they had come to pay homage to a great spirit, to one who had left behind him "the best things a man can leave: the reputation of friendship, of sonship, of devotion to his home and to his church . . . To his people I would say that this hour is one of pride in him, his life, and his character, rather than sorrow for his passing."

The substantial sum of £453 had been subscribed, some of it through a vaudeville concert at the Cremorne Theatre in Brisbane in which Australian middleweight boxer Ron Richards gave a sparring exhibition, and Phyl and her brother danced. Further money (£182) was raised through a fast-scoring match between two star-studded sides at the Sydney Cricket Ground, whose ground staff worked voluntarily (507 runs in four hours: Charlie Macartney 64, Tommy Andrews 77, Bill Brown 71, Don Bradman 98 [c Macartney b Mailey]).

After the purchase of the memorial stone the residue, £357, was handed to Archie's parents.

The Balmain club set up an Archie Jackson Memorial Shield award for the most successful of its grade teams each season. The initial winners were the 2nd XI in 1933-34.

Two years passed before, in February 1935, as the New South Wales players entered the dressing-room at the Brisbane Cricket Ground before their match with Queensland, they found a photograph of Archie on the dining table together with a bowl of fragrant roses—placed there by Phyl Thomas to commemorate the second anniversary of their engagement. There was a momentary hush as the players dumped their cricket bags. Out of the blue it was a time for memories.

Phyl later married and became a mother. An utterly charming lady, she died in Orange on September 3, 2001 at the age of 89. Her son, Bruce Kennedy, said that "like many of her vintage she spoke often of the 'old days'."

There were all sorts of reasons for remembering Archie Jackson. A boy from North Sydney recalled the trouble taken by him in 1930 after he had sent him an autograph book with the request that both the Australia and West Indies teams should sign it. The book was lost, so the boy wrote again. Jackson bought a fresh book, had it signed, and kept up a cordial correspondence for the remaining months of his life.

The second coming of Trumper had been short-lived, but the course of cricket history was changed by a few degrees. When Jackson's summers were gone forever, men, women and children were left to grieve. A torrent of words tumbled forth in the impossible attempt to pay justice to the young man and his deeds. Then life went on again, almost as before, leaving only the photographs, grey columns of prose, a few handwritten letters, and, over a plot of Australia's hard brown earth, a gravestone on which the inscription proclaims with beautiful simplicity: "He played the game".

ACKNOWLEDGEMENTS

The research and writing of this stirring but ultimately heart-breaking story of an Australian batting genius could not have been achieved today; not in such sharp detail anyway. The first edition of *Archie Jackson: the Keats of Cricket*, published in 1974, incorporated much personal detail that only Archie Jackson's family and team-mates and friends could have disclosed, well beyond the field of newspapers, magazines and books. Those people are no longer here, but they did share the pleasure of seeing their brother, their friend, their loved one remembered so many years after his death plunged Australia into a pit of grief.

The input from Archie's staunch boyhood friend Bill Hunt is clearly evident. So too is that of his sisters Peggie Jackson and Jean Bruce, and of his fiancée Phyl Kennedy (née Thomas). Among his contemporary cricketers in Sydney, Alan Kippax, skipper and mentor, gave generously of his memories just before he died, as did Bert Oldfield, Frank Buckle, Hunter "Stork" Hendry, and Bill O'Reilly. The vigilance of my dear friend in Queensland, Pat Mullins, led to the discovery of much interesting detail from his vast collection. Adelaide was out of reach, but letters to spin-bowling genius Clarrie Grimmett brought thoughtful replies.

Archie Jackson's English friend in Hampshire, genial farmer Harry Mills, contributed an important insight from correspondence retained through forty years. Harry read the original text of this book in typescript, but died before its publication. He was an especially good man, so like his young cricketer friend from Sydney.

Among pre-war England cricketers, R.E.S. (Bob) Wyatt, Herbert Sutcliffe, Leslie Ames, Ian Peebles, and George Geary all spoke glowingly of the young Australian, and I am indebted to all of them (now all gone) for significant substantiations.

A very considerable amount of fresh material has been added to the first edition of this biography, which was released in 1974, and we acknowledge the photograph of Archie Jackson batting against Victoria at Sydney in 1927-28, supplied by Michael Down.

It was a joy to have a foreword from England's famous fast bowler Harold Larwood, who by 1974 had long been a contented resident of Sydney. He retained enormous admiration for young Jackson, bordering on worship, which is rare for any opponent.

DAVID FRITH
Guildford, Surrey,
January 2020

Tribute: "He flashed across the cricket skies like a meteor. We had not realized, to the full, the brilliancy of his art when suddenly he was gone, but he left cricket the richer for his brief sojourn. He left, too, memories that we will cherish of a truly great batsman and a splendid sportsman."—Johnnie Moyes, *The Sun*, February 1933.

A Genius: Don Bradman, a pallbearer at Archie Jackson's funeral, declared his old teammate to be "a batting genius".

Index

OTHER BOOKS BY DAVID FRITH

Runs in the Family (with John Edrich), 1969

"My Dear Victorious Stod": a Biography of A.E. Stoddart, 1970 and 1977

The Archie Jackson Story, 1974 and 1987

The Fast Men, 1975

Cricket Gallery (ed.), 1975

Great Moments in Cricket (as 'Andrew Thomas'; with Norman Harris), 1976

England v Australia: A Pictorial History of the Test Matches Since 1877, (12 editions between 1977 and 2008)

The Ashes '77, (with Greg Chappell)

The Golden Age of Cricket 1890-1914, 1978

The Illustrated History of Test Cricket (ed. with Martin Tyler), 1978

The Ashes '79, 1979

Thommo (with Jeff Thomson), 1979

Rothmans Presents 100 Years England v Australia (co-editor), 1980

The Slow Men, 1984

Cricket's Golden Summer: Paintings in a Garden (with Gerry Wright), 1985

England v Australia Test Match Records 1877-1985 (editor)

Pageant of Cricket, 1987

Guildford Jubilee 1938-1988, 1988

By His Own Hand, 1990

Stoddy's Mission: the First Great Test Series 1894-95, 1995

Test Match Year 1996-97 (editor), 1997

Caught England, Bowled Australia [autobiography], 1997

The Trailblazers: the First English Cricket Tour of Australia 1861-62, 1999

Silence of the Heart: Cricket's Suicides, 2001

Bodyline Autopsy, 2002

The Ross Gregory Story, 2003

Battle for the Ashes 2005, 2005

The Battle Renewed: the Ashes Regained 2006-2007, 2007

Inside Story: Unlocking Australian Cricket's Archives (with Gideon Haigh), 2008

The David Frith Archive Catalogue, 2009

Frith on Cricket: Half a Century of Cricket Writing, 2010

Cricket's Collectors, 2012

Guildford's Cricket Story, 2013

Frith's Encounters, 2014

'Stoddy': England's Finest Sportsman, 2015

Touring with Bradman: Alec Hurwood's 1930 Diary, 2019

The Stoddart biography and *Pageant of Cricket* and *The Ross Gregory Story* each won the annual Cricket Society Book Award; Bodyline Autopsy was Wisden's Book of the Year and runner-up in the William Hill Sports Book of 2002, and early in 2010 cricketweb.net named it as Cricket Book of the Decade. David Frith was British Magazine Sportswriter of the Year 1988 (Sports Council) and Wombwell Cricket Lovers Society's Cricket Writer of the Year 1984. *Inside Story* won the Australian Cricket Society's 2008 Cricket Book of the Year award. Frith had five titles in *The Fifty Best Australian Cricket Books of All Time* (Ronald Cardwell and Roger Page, 2006). Two years later only Frith had as many as four books in Espncricinfo's Top 45 of all time, compiled by Suresh Menon.